HEMINGWAY'S
HURRICANE

———⊛⊛⊛———

"All our ignorance brings
us nearer to death."

T. S. ELIOT

———⊛⊛⊛———

HEMINGWAY'S HURRICANE

The Great Florida Keys
Storm of 1935

PHIL SCOTT

INTERNATIONAL MARINE / McGRAW-HILL

CAMDEN, MAINE • NEW YORK • CHICAGO

SAN FRANCISCO • LISBON • LONDON • MADRID

MEXICO CITY • MILAN • NEW DELHI • SAN JUAN

SEOUL • SINGAPORE • SYDNEY • TORONTO

1 2 3 4 5 6 7 8 9 DOC DOC 9 8 7 6 5

Cataloging-in-Publication Data is available
from the Library of Congress

ISBN 0-07-145332-6

Maps by International Mapping.

CONTENTS

CONTENTS

To Krista

FOREWORD

Start with 100,000 cubic miles of luxuriant tropical air, juicy with the humidity from a vacationer's dream of summery ocean waters. Stir it with coalescing thunderstorms and a hint of Coriolis force, just enough to shrug that inconceivable tonnage of airy mass into a spin. Keep the wind shear low to tighten the clouds' organization. Let thermodynamics loosen the brakes: the hot air rises, the surface pressure falls, and the spin accelerates. Rain pours down but the clouds inhale fresh water vapor even faster. Now the saturated moving air is a vast heat engine, and what was a sailor's idyll has become a monster consuming the sky, ripping at the sea. Hot, impatient wind racing twice as fast as a freight train obliterates everything in its way.

Most Americans don't know what a hurricane is. The word is familiar to us; from television reports and newspaper photographs we know of the devastation that these storms can bring; but we have never experienced one firsthand. Born in the Atlantic, hurricanes typically follow northwesterly paths through the Gulf of Mexico or fishhook through the

Florida peninsula before riding the jet stream northeast. Some skirt North America as long as possible and put off landfall until reaching the Carolinas or above. Because hurricanes draw all their fury from the lukewarm waters of the tropics and coastal shallows, their power dissipates rapidly as they cross dry land. So only a few millions of people along the southern rim and eastern edge of the United States get even a taste of what a hurricane can be.

The ones who do live where hurricanes roam can, over several decades, get to know dozens of them. Perhaps some of the milder storms will blur together in memory. But a few—the worst—will be unforgettable because of the carnage they cause. Hurricane Andrew in 1992, which demolished $30 billion worth of property. Deadly Hurricane Camille in 1969, which killed 172. And of course the legendary storm that Phil Scott describes here, the one that struck the Florida Keys on Labor Day weekend of 1935, the most intense hurricane in U.S. history.

Powerful as a hurricane is, one might not think that it needs help to do damage. But of course, where no one builds or travels, there is nothing man-made to wreck or human to kill. And so hurricanes are abetted by our ambition, our recklessness, our misjudgment, our stupidity, our greed, our cowardice. It is no small thing, however, that even in the maw of nature's gargantuan energies, some people still find the force of their own bravery, compassion, and strength.

Phil Scott has brilliantly and compellingly captured the events surrounding that 1935 storm, and pointed out how the

FOREWORD

human factors compounded the awful force of the sky and
sea. In that less-media-filled era, even fewer Americans had
the opportunity to see what a hurricane was. This is the story
of people who found out in the worst possible way, with
the worst possible storm, often in the very last seconds of
their lives.

— JOHN RENNIE, EDITOR IN CHIEF,
Scientific American

SOUTH FLORIDA IN 1935

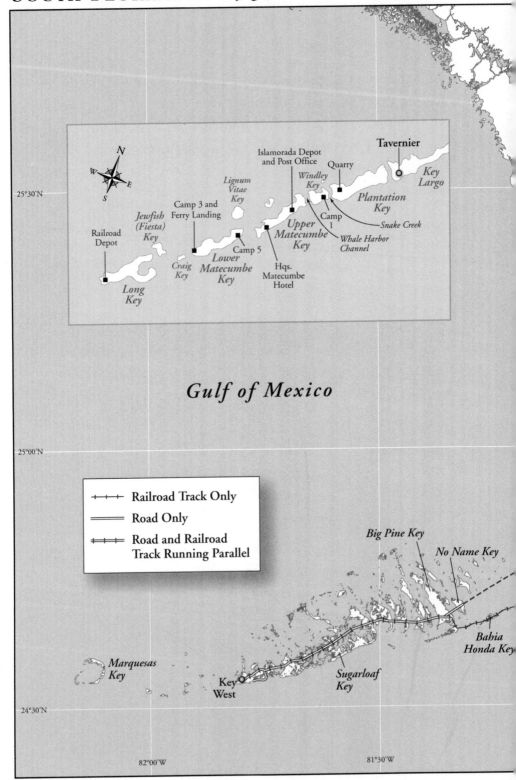

Tavernier

Islamarada Depot
and Post Office   Quarry

Windley
Key

Key
Largo

Plantation
Key

Camp
1

Snake Creek

Lignum
Vitae
Key

Camp 3 and
Ferry Landing

Upper
Matecumbe
Key

Whale Harbor
Channel

Jewfish
(Fiesta)
Key

Railroad
Depot

Craig
Key

Camp 5

Lower
Matecumbe
Key

Hqs.
Matecumbe
Hotel

Long
Key

N
W   E
S

Gulf of Mexico

25°30'N

25°00'N

+—+—+ Railroad Track Only

══════ Road Only

+══+══+ Road and Railroad
Track Running Parallel

Big Pine Key

No Name Key

Bahia
Honda Key

Marquesas
Key

Key
West

Sugarloaf
Key

24°30'N

82°00'W   81°30'W

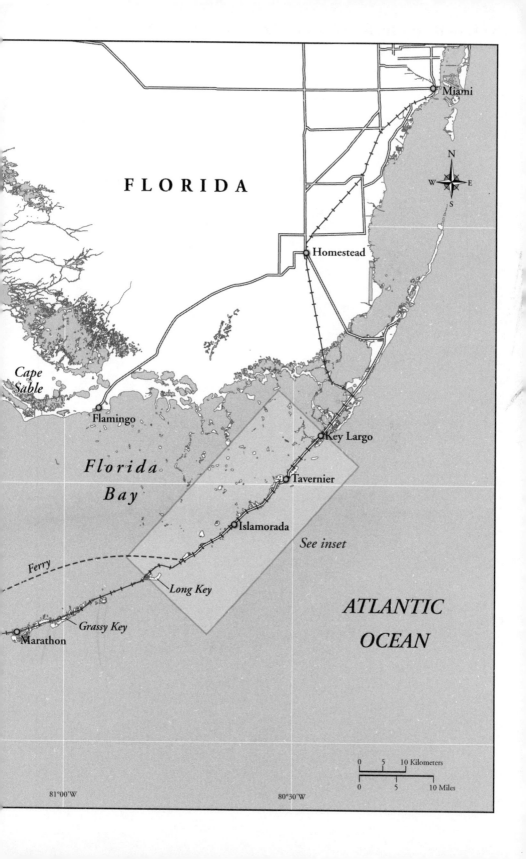

THE PATH OF THE HURRICANE AS REPORTED BY THE U.S. WEATHER SERVICE

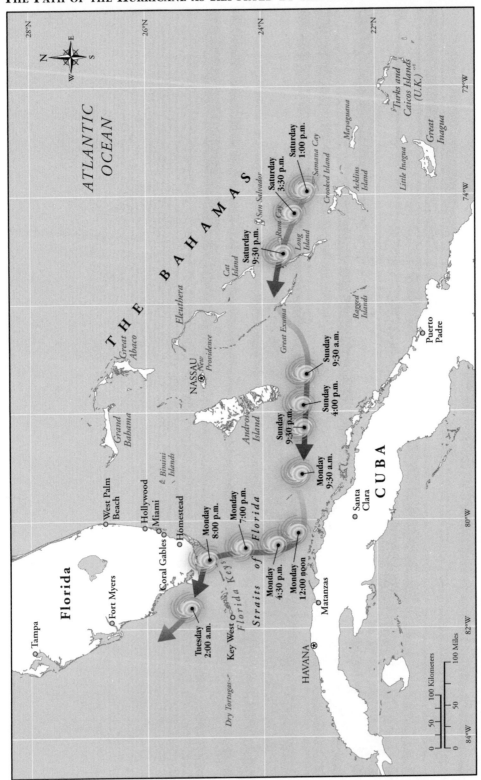

PROLOGUE

Saturday
August 31, 1935

As he did every other day, Ernest Hemingway rose early in the bright, sunny bedroom of his yellow stucco, Spanish-style mansion on the southeast corner of Olivia and Whitehead streets in Key West. He pulled on his well-stained Basque shorts, tied the rope around his waist that he used for a belt, and slipped on his sandals. Then he padded across the second-story walkway that tied the house to his office—the mansion's former carriage house—and sat down in his Cuban cigar maker's chair.

There Hemingway picked up a fresh pencil and, after a time, wrote approximately 500 words of a short story. He wrote about that much each morning. Sometimes he did more, sometimes less; if planning an overnight trip fishing, he tried to write twice as much.

As always, when he was finished he recorded the exact number of words and the date on a piece of paper taped next to the window in front of the old gateleg table he used as a desk. The window looked out through palm trees and tropical plants nearly covering the nearby weather-beaten gray wooden shacks whose sloping roofs drained rainwater to cisterns, the Keys' only source of fresh water. Beyond them he saw the sea, the surf beating calmly against what beach there was along the rocky shore. The sea had been beating on that shore for thousands of years, and would for thousands more.

Finished writing, Hemingway had his first drink. He was a serious drinking man—in a future demonstration of temperance he would write to his editor, Max Perkins, "Have given up nearly all morning drinking"—but despite the fact that Prohibition had been repealed by Franklin Delano Roosevelt two years before, he was not a Democrat. Hemingway despised the President. He saw FDR as "very Harvard charming and sexless and womanly, seems like a great woman Secretary of Labor, say." He thought even less of the New Deal; to him it was socialism. "Some sort of YMCA show," he wrote. "Starry eyed bastards spending money that somebody will have to pay. Everybody in our town quit to go on relief. Fishermen all turned carpenters."

In the 1830s, sea trade had made Key West the richest city per capita in the country. In 1922 the town's population had reached 22,000, but by 1935 Key West was bankrupt and its population had plummeted to 12,500. To save it, Florida's state government hoped to turn Hemingway's adopted town into a tourist destination, and had appealed to the federal government for help.

Hemingway and his second wife, Pauline Pfeiffer, had bought the house in 1931, a ramshackle, limestone two-story on one and a half acres. It had been built in the nineteenth century by shipping magnate Asa Tift, whose workmen had carved it from white coral "keystone" quarried on the property itself. That hole formed a basement, rare in the Keys, and the hard, thick keystone walls also made it one of the few hurricane-proof houses in Key West. And because Hemingway lived there, FDR's Florida man, Julius Stone—head of the Florida Emergency Relief Administration, the state branch of the Federal Emergency Relief Administration—had put the mansion on tourist maps. Hemingway hated Julius Stone too.

Toby Brice, a jack-of-all-trades who would design the cover of Hemingway's next book, *For Whom the Bell Tolls,* and a handyman out of necessity, had constructed an undulating six-foot-high wall from paving bricks in early 1935 to keep Hemingway's sons in and sightseers out. Brice built an ugly wall, but it satisfied the writer.

Safe behind his brick wall Saturday afternoon (after taking lunch, or more accurately a late breakfast, at the Electric Kitchen on Fleming Street), Hemingway read the *Key West Citizen,* which reported a tropical disturbance 800 miles southeast. The wind wasn't strong yet, but it was freshening a bit, and the clouds low on the horizon looked dark and heavy with rain. From a nautical chart, he calculated that the storm—

if it became one—would eventually hit Key West, and so he made a mental note to prepare the house the next day and then walk over to the Key West Navy Yard, where he kept his 38-foot boat, *Pilar*, his wife's nickname and the name he would use for a strong character in *For Whom the Bell Tolls*.

Stowing his charts, he sauntered down the street to Sloppy Joe's and started drinking with a few of the indigent veterans from the federal camps to the north, on the Matecumbe Keys. They'd taken the train to Key West for the Labor Day Weekend.

Hemingway's contempt for the unemployed and the federal work relief programs was overridden by his love of swapping war stories with veterans. They called him "Hem," just like his friends in Paris had a decade earlier. They gave him a couple of other nicknames too: "Old Master," for one, and "Mahatma," because he liked to wrap a towel around his head in the late-August heat. He had too much belly fat to resemble Mahatma Gandhi, though, or for that matter any of the veterans, who had seen the specter of starvation close-up. Hours later he finished his last drink and weaved his way in the dark back home to Whitehead Street.

Ernest Hemingway had no way of knowing, on this Saturday before the Great Hurricane, what lasting alterations the storm would make in the fabric of his life.

CHAPTER ONE

Friday
August 30, 1935
Florida Keys

Joseph Fecteau drove his Chevy pickup truck north along
the dusty highway from Camp 5 to his home on Upper
Matecumbe Key, where he and six other World War I veterans had built shacks barely large enough to accommodate
the families they hoped would soon be joining them from
up North. Other families had arrived already, but Fecteau
was still waiting for his wife and daughters. He'd just collected his August wages of $36 from the paymaster in Camp 5
and had to send a large portion of it to his wife in Washington, D.C. What was left would have to stretch over a whole
month, so he had little choice but to spend the long Labor
Day weekend on the Key.

Born in Massachusetts, Fecteau—or "Frenchy," as men had called him since boot camp almost twenty years earlier—was thin, wiry, and tall. In contrast to the other veterans, who typically wore blue dungarees and blue shirts, he dressed in whites, because he worked at the camp headquarters in the Matecumbe Hotel. He made the three-mile drive from Camp 5, much of it over the causeway connecting the Upper and Lower Matecumbes, the Atlantic spread out on his right, the Florida Bay and the Gulf of Mexico to the left. The breeze through the open windows of his truck gave Frenchy a reprieve from the oppressive heat, which took away his desire to breathe, and from the oily stench of rotting small animal corpses that were forever baking in the pitiless sun.

If he noticed it at all, one thing looked strange: small crabs were scuttling from the Atlantic side across the road toward the Gulf of Mexico. Keys residents, who called themselves Conchs, knew after two or three generations of clinging to their sea-swept limestone outcrops that crabs behaved that way just ahead of a hurricane.

Frenchy had served in the Great War as a pilot on the Western Front, flying canvas-covered wooden-framed biplanes above no-man's-land a scant fifteen years after the Wright brothers' first flight. He wasn't a hero like America's ace, Eddie Rickenbacker. In fact he was no hero at all. He had never shot down an enemy aircraft, never distinguished himself in combat in any way. As it would any sane man, wartime flying had frightened him. A pilot could be killed by "Archie"—as the German antiaircraft shells timed to explode at an airplane's altitude were called—and when they did, shards of metal ripped apart the wings, the fuselage, and even the pilot. Then there were the fighter planes. They dove on you from behind or from out of the sun. If their machine guns hit the engine, a fuel tank, or fuel line, a guy had no choice but to ride the flaming plane down or jump to a certain death. No pilot wore a parachute; commanders on both sides thought it might encourage airmen to leap before engaging the enemy.

The average life span for an active-duty pilot on the Western Front had been three weeks. Somehow, Fecteau had made it through almost a year flying combat above the Marne, the Meuse-Argonne, and the Belleau Woods. At eleven o'clock on November 11, 1918—Armistice Day—the firing stopped. The generals found the symmetry of 11.11.11 amusing. No one could accuse them of being humorless about war.

But the veterans did not find it amusing when, returning to the States, they found their jobs filled and had to start all over again. And then, when some of them finally began to find their footing, the Great Depression came along. By the 1930s their average age had been about forty-one, but most of the war veterans looked fifteen or twenty years older. They were broken down and poorly dressed, with bad teeth, poor health, and empty stomachs.

The war had left its mark. Years later, many of them lived in fear. Physicians called their condition "shell shock," thinking it was caused by the sudden percussive pressure of shells exploding nearby. But they misdiagnosed it.

Shell shock was not a physical malady at all, but a psychological response to the horrors of combat. No one knew when one of those black bursts of Archie would explode too close, rip off your tail or wings, and send your biplane plummeting out of control. Archie could shoot black slivers of metal through your body. In open cockpits at 18,000 feet, gasping thin air at 30 degrees below zero, pilots suffered both hypoxia and hypothermia. Flying was a tough, short straw to draw.

But it was positively romantic duty compared with being an infantryman in the trenches. Shell shock there rooted itself in terror and deafness as exploding shells spattered the face of a young man—no more than a boy, really—with mud and the bloody bits of men who only seconds before had been crouched nearby, trying to make themselves small. Shell shock germinated in slogs through the knee-deep mud and barbed wire of no-man's-land while enemy machine gunners mowed down companions so fast that only one in twenty-seven actually made it far enough to jump into an enemy trench. And shell shock flourished in the complete and utter exhaustion of days, weeks, and months of sleepless combat on the front; in constant exposure to heat and cold and rain; and in the ever-present stench of mustard gas and rotting corpses. Perhaps worst of all, a man could be wracked by guilt, the guilt of surviving while all around him buddies were dying, their heads blown open or their blood draining from gaping wounds.

Shell shock would go on growing even after a soldier returned home. He might nod off, and his dreams would consist of little but combat, so he'd try not to sleep. Sometimes he might relive the explosions and screams during his waking hours, or overreact when an automobile backfired and become hysterical, hitting the ground as if under attack. He might lose his appetite for food and sex, distance himself from friends and family, withdraw emotionally from everyday activities and the world around him.

In World War II, Army psychiatrists would give shell shock a new name: combat fatigue. Soldiers would call it "Nervous in the Service" and pray that it wouldn't happen to them. General George Patton would famously slap a man for it and then make a reluctant public apology.

Later still, the condition would be called "post-traumatic stress syndrome," followed by the judgment-neutral "post-traumatic stress disorder." But regardless of the label, the results were the same. Any trauma, terror, accident, or natural disaster could trigger it. Without treatment, the internal combat could go on for years, to be halted only by death.

For two decades, shell-shocked veterans of the Great War had been kicked from pillar to post with no recognition that they suffered from a mental illness. A few of the more severe cases had been reduced to one-syllable words.

Shell shock still plagued Frenchy Fecteau seventeen years after the war. After returning from Europe, he had bounced from one truck-driving job to another. Eventually he found work in Washington, D.C., driving for the Baltimore Transfer Company, but then the Great Depression hit and things got really tough.

The Depression began with the stock market crash of 1929, and sank to new depths in 1932, when the unemployment rate in America reached an astonishing 29.4 percent. Nearly one-third of all people found themselves out of work. Fecteau was laid off from Baltimore Transfer and had no money to support his wife and kids.

———— ❧ ————

That year, it seemed as though the entire world was going to hell.

Historians identify an Age of Faith and an Age of Reason. Surely, then, the 1930s began the Age of Tyranny. The Great Depression gripped the entire world, and widespread poverty led inevitably to dictatorship. In Germany, 6 million were unemployed and thousands rioted in the Berlin streets. In 1932, the Nazi Party, led by Austrian-born Adolf Hitler, won a stunning majority of the seats in the German Reichstag, and in 1933 Hitler was appointed chancellor. The weak, democratic Weimar Republic, which had replaced Kaiser Wilhelm after the war, collapsed soon afterward. In the USSR, as part of his second Five-Year Plan, dictator Joseph Stalin increased the grain quota in the Ukraine by 44 percent, with the proviso that no peasants could consume any before they filled the quota; by 1932 nearly 10 million starved to death. In Italy, Benito Mussolini's Fascist army was so successful in its war against Ethiopia that the African country's only European ally, France, declared it could no longer offer support. In 1932, Japan launched an overwhelming offensive against Shanghai, and China's Chiang Kai-shek could do little to stop it.

One haunting popular song, written in 1932 by Yip Harburg and Jay Gourney and recorded by Bing Crosby and then Rudy Vallee, summed up the American experience:

> Once I built a railroad, made it run,
> Made it race against time.
> Once I built a railroad, now it's done.
> Buddy, can you spare a dime?

Nature, not tyranny, caused much suffering in isolationist America. In the Midwest the rain simply stopped falling. Wind rolled over farmland and picked up the dry topsoil, creating massive black blizzards that blew choking dust at 60 miles per hour and buried small towns in a thick layer of dirt. People there called it the Dirty Thirties. The drought left 50 million acres unable to support crops. There were no jobs in the cities, in small towns, on the farms, anywhere. There was no unemployment insurance, no social security. Instead there were breadlines, eight men wide, a mile long. Tens of thousands from the Midwest to the Great Plains—like the Joad clan in John Steinbeck's *Grapes of Wrath*—headed west on Highway 66 toward California, the promised land, with its truck farms and its rumor of jobs. They arrived to signs that said OKIE, GO HOME.

If there was one hope for any veteran, it was the War Bonus. Voted by Congress in 1924, overriding President Coolidge's veto, the bonus of $1.25 for each day a veteran had served overseas was to be paid in 1945.

Walter Waters had seen his share of slaughter as a medic for the 146th Field Artillery, participating in the battles of Château-Thierry, Aisne-Marne, Saint-Mihiel, and Meuse-Argonne. After the war he'd gone from job to job, finally working at a Portland, Oregon, cannery. But he lost his job early in 1932. That March, at a meeting of the National Veterans Association in Portland, the thin, ragged veteran rose from his chair to speak. Waters told the men that they should travel to Washington, D.C., and demand early payment of their war bonus. With conditions this bad, he said, they needed that money right away. His fellow veterans ignored him at that meeting, but Waters kept giving speeches, and by May, when a bill proposing to pay the bonus was shot down by Congress, the Portland veterans decided that a march on Washington sounded like a good idea. They voted to form an army of sorts, the Bonus Expeditionary Force, echoing the name of the American Expeditionary Force that had sailed to Europe's rescue in 1917. Three hundred of them blocked the tracks of the Union Pacific Railroad nearby and commandeered the first freight train that came along. Eighteen days later the Bonus Expeditionary Force rode into Washington, picking up veterans along the way. They made camp inside a vacant federal building across the Potomac River, voted Waters their general, then marched in peaceful ranks around the Capitol and the White House.

Word got out through newspapers, newsreels, radio, and word of mouth, and in no time their number swelled to more than 20,000 poor, tired, and hungry veterans, the wretched refuse of America. They came from the Dust Bowl of the Midwest, from failed tenant farms down South and migrant workers scraping a living in fields, and from the dead and dying factories of the North. They came from everywhere and from nowhere in particular, by boxcar and on foot, in jalopies and trucks, and they brought their families with them. The new influx of Bonus Marchers settled into more vacant government buildings and nearby parks in hastily constructed cardboard shantytowns that were dubbed Hoovervilles, after Republican President Herbert Hoover. There were Hoovervilles all over the country—the pathetic cardboard concoctions of rootless, dispossessed squatters—but to see them practically from the White House windows was a deep embarrassment for the president.

Hoover didn't want to pay out the $2.4 billion that Congress had appropriated for veterans in 1924, nor did he want to be seen supporting the rebellious marchers. But he quietly gave the vets Army blankets, field kitchens, and a dispensary staffed by government personnel. The Bonus Marchers continued adding to their numbers, and by June 25,000 lived in twenty-seven camps. Among them were Communists, whose antigovernment agitation the BEF leaders largely ignored, yet whose very presence alarmed the Hoover administration.

On June 15 the bonus issue went to the floor of the House of Representatives. As the debate proceeded, 10,000 veterans smoked, milled about, and lay down in front of the Capitol building. Finally, Waters emerged from the dome to shout that the House had voted 209 to 176 to give the marchers their bonus.

On June 17 the bill went to the Senate, and again thousands of BEF men stood outside, anxiously awaiting the results. But the Senate voted it down, 62–18. The press predicted riots, but on Waters's command the men, 12,000 strong, began singing "God Bless America" in the evening air. Then they quietly walked back to their camps and abandoned buildings.

As June gave way to hot, muggy July, several thousand Bonus Marchers left Washington to make it home as best they could, and Hoover quietly sponsored a bill for $100,000 to pay their way out of the city. But Waters vowed, "We'll stay till 1945!" and 8,000 kept his promise. Some took over even more government buildings, this time inside Washington itself. Congress gave them until July 15 to leave, and then the police were sent out to Camp Anacostia—as the BEF called their Hooverville on the far side of the Anacostia Bridge, south of the Capitol and the center of the city—to disperse the veterans. At that point the former soldiers' old training kicked in and they pushed the police back across the bridge and pressed on into the city, throwing bricks and rocks. The police fired back with guns, but when the dust settled, the attack on Camp Anacostia had been repulsed. Hoover, under pressure from Army Chief of Staff Douglas MacArthur, felt he had no other choice. He called out the Army—and General MacArthur himself.

Later, Hoover claimed that he'd ordered MacArthur to take it easy on the BEF, but the temperamental, autocratic general ignored the qualms of his president and the objections of his aide, Major Dwight D. Eisenhower, and mounted a full offensive. His troops fought the veterans back to the Anacostia Bridge with tear gas and bayonets, and then the cavalry appeared, led by Major George S. Patton, brandishing swords and shooting guns. Bullets killed two Bonus Marchers, and the Army plowed five tanks through the cardboard Hoovervilles and flattened them, smothering one baby. Finally the soldiers set the Hoovervilles on fire, scattering the BEF for good.

For putting down the protest, Congress awarded MacArthur his second Distinguished Service Medal. He had earned his first one leading those same ragged veterans across Europe in the Great War.

Armed troops firing on veterans contributed little to Herbert Hoover's public image. That November, he lost the national election in a landslide to New York's Democratic governor, Franklin Delano Roosevelt, who had promised a New Deal for all Americans when he accepted his party's nomination. The old deal, which included the Army shooting its own veterans, wasn't working anymore.

Economic conditions improved a little after Roosevelt's "First Hundred Days" in office, as the initial flurry of a newly elected president has since often been called. But 3,000 veterans marched on Washington in 1933, and 1,500 in 1934. Roosevelt sent coffee wagons and his wife, Eleanor, to meet them. When the veterans gathered again in 1935, Roosevelt and his administration concocted a better plan. Although Supreme Court Justice Oliver Wendell Holmes slammed FDR as "a second-class intellect with a first-class temperament," the politically savvy New Yorker knew he needed to defuse this recurring protest before it took root. "Shrewd Franklin Roosevelt never let his Bonus Marchers get the Washington spotlight," *Time* magazine wrote. "Quick as querulous down-at-heels veterans began shuffling into Washington he began shipping them off to special relief camps in the South."

FDR also firmly believed that the unemployed wanted—needed—the dignity of work instead of a public handout. The man whom Roosevelt had placed in charge of all public works programs, Federal Emergency Relief Administration director Harry Hopkins, was instrumental in devising a slew of ever-evolving organizations to deal with the massive numbers of unemployed. FERA itself distributed $500 million to states and municipalities for public works projects, but that was just the beginning. People had their choice of so-called alphabet soup employment organizations under Hopkins's aegis.

The earliest of these was the Civilian Conservation Corps, or CCC, signed into law on March 31, 1933, during Roosevelt's First Hundred Days blitzkrieg. Its workers were referred to as the C's, and the public nicknamed it the Tree Army. A half-million young men between the ages of eighteen and twenty-four enlisted by 1935, plus a few thousand World War I veterans. Men joined up because, like the Bonus Army, they were hungry and homeless, or pretty close to it, and the Corps gave them their keep—"three hots and a cot," as soldiers called it, and clothes if needed—plus $30 a month. They got to pocket $5, and the Corps sent the rest back home to their families.

The boys signed up for a six-month stint and could re-up three times. They spent their days in the outdoors, building campgrounds and trails, parklands and roads. They planted a checkerboard of trees in the Dust Bowl to prevent soil erosion. Of all FDR's alphabet administrations, the CCC gained the most popularity with Republicans, the boys who were in it, and the public in general. Maybe that was because the CCC was the first work relief program bestowed on a frightened, weary nation, or perhaps it was because small towns profited from the young men spending their allowance money without much hell-raising.

The Works Progress Administration never achieved the CCC's acceptance. Formed by executive order on May 6, 1935, and headed by Harry Hopkins, the WPA paid older men $1 a day—just like the CCC—to build roads, bridges, and even government buildings. The work wasn't the point; getting money into desperate hands was. Detractors of these programs, which included nearly every staunch Republican and almost anyone else who still had a job, called the WPA workers "Shovel Leaners." Sometimes they called themselves Shovel Leaners.

When a project began, the WPA would overload it with workers who didn't have much to do or much incentive to do it. Some even figured that FDR wanted a standing army of sorts, like Hitler's Brown Shirts, whom his party would pay to keep voting him into office, an American dictator. The Shovel Leaners, though, built most of the roads and bridges crisscrossing America before President Eisenhower's Federal Highway project was begun in the 1950s. They built Boulder (later Hoover) Dam and the recreation area that would one day be known as Camp David. They constructed the dams of the Tennessee Valley Authority, and they built the Golden Gate Bridge. And WPA leaders strongly encouraged folks who joined to look for employment elsewhere—a person's stint might last only a month or two if he could find another job.

Before heading the WPA, in his last months leading FERA, Harry Hopkins helped organize yet another relief initiative, this one aimed at World War I veterans. FERA created veterans' work camps across the South that were modeled after CCC camps but with state oversight. Among the men sent to build and populate these so-called veterans' rehabilitation camps were the Bonus Marchers in Washington, and about 700 of them ended up in three work camps in the Florida Keys.

On a map, the Keys resemble an unclasped jade bracelet dangling 130 miles south and west from the state's eastern edge. In all, nearly four hundred major and minor Keys sprinkle Florida's southern seas. Geographers once believed them to be the descending tail end of the 230-million-year-old Appalachian Mountains. The Keys, though, are not so ancient as that; they were formed nearly 30 million years ago when the Atlantic Ocean began rising and sinking in response to the freezing and melting of northern glaciers. When the Keys surfaced for the last time some 30,000 years ago, their base consisted of bedrock that was slowly covered with a thick, heavy layer of limestone, which in turn has been covered with coral and silt and the shells of small sea creatures. The Keys are low-lying, near sea level. One of the northern islands, Windley Key, perches 18 feet above sea level, but the average Key tops out just 5 feet above the Atlantic.

The environment encountered by early visitors and residents was a simple one. Just offshore lay the sea-grass community. On the shoreline fringe grew mangrove swamps, followed by a "transition zone," then hardwoods like plane and poisonwood trees. The shallower, southern islands were underlain by Miami oolite, which supported especially thick vegetation, but all the Keys were densely vegetated, impenetrable to humans and to most animals larger than the tiny Key deer. Between four and seven miles offshore in the Atlantic, stretching from Key Largo past Key West, lay North

America's sole living coral reef. Teeming with sea life, the reef also put up a barrier that kept the Atlantic from grinding away the Keys. But it left few beaches.

On one Key in the 1500s, the Spaniards found the manchineel tree, which exudes a deadly white sap. They also found that the Key Indians, forerunners of the Seminoles, would dip their arrows and other battle accoutrements into the sap and attack the Conquistadors. And so the Spanish named that Key "Matecumbe," from the Spanish *mate hombre*, "kill man."

<hr>

Down the spine of the Keys in 1935, from Miami to Key West, ran the old Flagler Overseas Railway, part of the Florida East Coast Railway. Before the railroad declared bankruptcy in 1932, newspapers described it as the Eighth Wonder of the World. They also called it "Flagler's Folly."

The railroad was the brainchild of Henry Morrison Flagler, a veritable force of nature. Born in Hopewell, New York, in 1830, the son of a minister, Flagler took himself to Bellevue, Ohio, at age fourteen, and found work in a grain store. At nineteen he became a grain salesman, earning $400 per month. In 1862 he moved to Saginaw, Michigan, where he mined salt as a preservative from recently discovered deposits nearby. Salt prices shot through the stratosphere during the Civil War, when the Union provisioned its massive army, and Flagler made a fortune. But prices collapsed after General Lee surrendered at Appomattox. Flagler, who didn't understand much about producing and selling salt anyway, found himself $50,000 ($1.17 million in 2003 dollars) in debt.

He left for Cleveland, started a grain business there, began paying off his creditors, and, significantly for him, settled on the same street as John D. Rockefeller. In 1862, Rockefeller had left the grain business to start his own company refining and selling oil, then used primarily as a lighting fuel and lubricant. Four years later Rockefeller's company had sales of $2 million, the equivalent of $45 million today. He and Flagler, who was nine years younger than Rockefeller, worked in the same building and walked home together, and by 1867 Rockefeller convinced Flagler to invest in what would become Standard Oil. Flagler, just barely out of debt, scraped together $100,000 from a relative on the condition that he become Rockefeller's partner, and in just a few years he grew extraordinarily rich. Standard Oil emerged as America's top refinery in 1872, producing 10,000 barrels a day, and in 1877, when the company moved its headquarters to New York, Flagler bought a home at 509 Fifth Avenue. Rumor placed his worth somewhere between $10 million and $20 million in 1880—nobody could say just how much. Flagler himself didn't seem to know.

Tall, stout, and well-dressed, as Flagler aged his hair and walrus mustache turned white. He fell in love with Florida the first time he laid eyes on it. He had ridden there in his private railroad car, Number 90, with his gravely ailing first wife, Mary, on the advice of her personal physician. Disembarking in Jacksonville, they were enchanted by the clean air, the Spanish architecture, the palm trees, the bright skies and sunny beaches. It was lush, even for paradise. Flagler found one major problem, though—a lack of infrastructure. Florida had hardly any cities and few luxury hotels, and most of its barely 480 miles of railroad track ran along the northeastern coast, stopping in Jacksonville.

After only a few weeks he got antsy and returned to New York and his growing wealth with his wife and two children. But Flagler's money and their weeks of respite in Florida weren't enough to cure Mary. When she died in May 1881, Flagler started reexamining his life. He retired as Standard Oil's treasurer at the age of fifty-three—though not from its board of directors—eventually remarried, and moved from New York to St. Augustine.

But despite announcing his retirement, Flagler couldn't slow down. What this lush paradise needed was someone to develop it, and Flagler figured he was that someone. Because there were few places fit to stay, he built luxurious hotels, purchased and upgraded others, and contributed money to the city of St. Augustine to build a new city hall and a new school for blacks. His grand, ornate Hotel Ponce de León (now part of Flagler College) was the world's largest concrete structure at the time of its building in 1887. He donated money to build the city's sewers, pave streets, and electrify the streetlights. He funded a new hospital and rebuilt the Catholic cathedral when it nearly burned to the ground. He started buying up railroads in and around St. Augustine, then branched out south along the coast.

Flagler built railroads to Daytona, then built railroad bridges to gap the rivers south of Daytona and laid more track farther down the coast. By 1894, Flagler's railroad reached a place he christened West Palm Beach, and his 1,150-room Royal Poinciana Hotel in Palm Beach became the world's largest wooden structure.

He might have stopped in West Palm Beach, but winter freezes in 1894 and 1895 lured him even farther south, and he drove his railroad to the backwater settlement that would become Miami in exchange for free land from commercial interests there, reaching Biscayne Bay in 1896 and opening the ritzy Royal Palm Hotel in 1897. Flagler dredged Miami's first shipping channel and financed its first roads, its first water and sewer systems, and its first newspaper, the *Metropolis*. In 1902 he moved into Whitehall, his 60,000-square-foot Palm Beach estate, a wedding gift to his third wife, Mary Lily.

When the Spanish-American War of 1898 rendered Cuba a U.S. protectorate, Flagler thought someone should open Cuba to trade. For this reason, and because Key West was then Florida's largest city and America's closest deepwater port to the Panama Canal, which the U.S. now controlled and was planning to finish, he determined to extend his railroad to Key West. In 1904, now seventy-four years old, Flagler approached J. C. Meredith, a young man who had just finished a magnificent pier at Tampico, Mexico, and was an acknowledged master of reinforced concrete. Flagler offered Meredith a job.

When Flagler announced his plan to George M. Ward, his pal replied, "Flagler, you need a guardian." Common folks derided the multimillion-dollar project, but they went south to work on it just the same. The pay was low—$1.25 per day—and they had to pay back the $12 Flagler advanced them from their wages to cover the fare down to Florida on his trains. They came from northern cities like Philadelphia and New York; most were derelicts and bums—hoboes recruited by labor agencies—who quit after their first paycheck and went on benders in Miami that lasted as long as the money did. Flagler also hired Cubans and Spaniards, and a few blacks from the Cayman Islands.

When engineers drew up plans for the Overseas Railway, they designed it with causeways—solid ramparts—spanning some of the open-water stretches between Key Largo and Key West. They solidified the track bed by covering a fill of marine marl with flint gravel. Starting out like mud, marl dries to a concrete hardness and will seldom wash out. It seemed a good idea, but two groups—Keys residents and the U.S. government—protested, saying that the causeways might dam up an incoming storm surge and flood the Keys. So the engineers redrew their plans to include six additional miles of bridgework. This satisfied the government, though not the Conchs, but the Conchs utterly lacked political clout.

Everything the construction crews needed at their camps scattered through the Keys, from concrete to food to medical supplies, Flagler had to ship in. He employed Mississippi River sternwheel paddle steamers and a fleet of tramp steamers to carry crushed rock and coal from the mainland.

He brought in barges and fourteen houseboats that could sleep up to 100 men each. Shoreside, he housed men in a series of camps, each with a mess hall and a free hospital. Each month the workers needed 4.5 million gallons of fresh water, which Flagler shipped down from Homestead twice daily on two special trains of flatbed cars, with two 7,000-gallon cypress tanks per car.

His company built camps for its construction workers throughout the Keys, and the engineers kept on working through the prime hurricane months, June through October. To warn themselves of impending storms, they built crude barometers from water-filled glass tubes that contained weeds drifting around on the bottom. When the air pressure dropped, signifying a tropical storm, the weeds floated higher.

On the night of October 17, 1906, the weeds stirred on the bottoms of the glass tubes, and early the following morning a narrow hurricane blew in from the southeast, slamming full force into the camp at Long Key, just south of the Matecumbes. The men there were quartered in two large Mississippi River cargo barges, with kitchen and dining areas in their high-sided hulls and bunkhouses fastened to their decks. Helpless without tugs to pull them, the barges could neither get farther out to sea nor onto land. By seven-thirty both barges' moorings snapped in the 100-mile-an-hour winds; by nine that morning the rocking houseboats began leaking, and heavy seas bashed planking from their sides and blew the houses from the decks. "Some men couldn't swim and were afraid of sharks," wrote William Sanders, chief engineer for a tugboat, who was bunked on Houseboat 4. "They drank laudanum from first-aid kits and lay down to die." One houseboat washed ashore, but Houseboat 4 drifted out into the Atlantic with 150 men aboard. Some were lucky enough to be rescued by ships, but 130 workers died out of the nearly 3,000 laboring at the time. It was the first hurricane of the young century to make landfall in Florida.

Worse yet for Flagler, much of his construction equipment was damaged or destroyed, and the Long Key viaduct itself, under construction at the lower end of the Key, was badly damaged. Still, Flagler refused to quit.

The following year, 1907, the weather was better, and Flagler kept the men carving the railroad down the center of the Keys. With 2,500 men working for them, engineers completed the 2.15-mile Long Key viaduct in January 1908. Spanning the waters to Conch Key, the viaduct required 286,000 barrels of cement, 177,000 cubic yards of gravel, 106,000 cubic yards of sand, 5,700 yards of reinforcing rod, 612,000 feet of pilings, and 2.6 million board feet of lumber. With 186 reinforced arches 35 feet wide, it stood 31 feet above high tide.

Flagler was so proud of the viaduct that he used it as the trademark of his Overseas Railway. On Long Key in 1908 he cut a swath of the shore back to its fringing palm trees and converted the construction camp to a fishing camp. By 1909 the camp included a two-story hotel and, according to the *Key West Citizen*, "30 neat little cottages," though Flagler's brochures claimed only fourteen. A winter vacation in the

tropics was the newest obsession of well-heeled northern-
ers, and the *Citizen* reported in February 1910 that "things
are humming in the Long Key Fishing Camp. Mackerel and
king fish are plentiful. So are the tourists." Soon, wealthy men
such as Zane Grey—who first visited Long Key in 1911—
would dock their yachts on the Gulf side and ride a narrow-
gauge tramcar under the Overseas Railway tracks to their cottages on the Atlantic shore. Herbert Hoover would visit there
in future years, and became an honorable member of the
Long Key Fishing Club, formed in 1917 with Zane Grey as first
president. FDR would also visit.

Meanwhile, construction continued unabated into the
Middle Keys, bypassing Duck Key, then crossing Grassy,
Crawl, and Vaca Keys. On Vaca Key the pace reached such
a hectic frenzy that one man observed, "Building this railroad
has become a regular marathon." According to legend, that's
how the settlement of Marathon got its name. By early 1908
the railroad reached its new terminus at Knight's Key Dock,
just south of Marathon, the halfway point to Key West, and
Flagler instituted twice-daily rail service from Miami.

At Knight's Key the crews prepared to build the impossible: the Seven Mile Bridge, which actually spanned nine
miles. The workers built it in four sections: Knight's Key
Bridge, the Pigeon Key Bridge, and the Moser Channel
Bridge, which were simple concrete foundations anchored to
the bedrock as deep as 28 feet beneath the water's surface.
On top they placed steel-girder spans, then they mounted a
swinging span 253 feet long to allow shipping to pass back

and forth between the Atlantic and the Gulf. For the final span to Bahia Honda Key, the Pacet Channel viaduct, they constructed a series of 210 concrete arches, 53 feet long, almost like the Long Key viaduct.

The following year, 1909, Meredith died from exhaustion, and his assistant, William Krome, moved into his place to extend the railroad from the Middle into the Lower Keys. As part of his initiation, that autumn another hurricane struck. This time the crews were prepared: telegraph wires reached to Miami for quick weather reports, and Flagler ordered all women to leave the camps at the start of hurricane season. The men left behind were housed in sturdy barracks of wood. But the storm hit hard, with winds reaching 125 miles per hour. In its aftermath, Miami telegraphed harsh news to the rest of the world: the storm had completely wiped out Flagler's railroad.

Luckily, the news was exaggerated. The hurricane wrought millions of dollars worth of damage that would set the project's completion back by two years; Flagler lost a lot of his floating equipment and miles of track, bridges, and embankment. By some accounts, forty men died. But all the concrete arches handily withstood wind forces that were four times greater than ever before recorded in the Keys.

Krome realized that the railroad needed more bridgework to survive the surges from future hurricanes of equal or greater strength, so he reengineered the remaining spans to incorporate three times as much. But he didn't back up and add more bridges in the Middle and Upper Keys.

While repairing the hurricane's damage, the workers kept on pushing the railroad south and west. In 1910 the next hurricane struck suddenly and without warning. A brutal storm, with winds that reached 125 miles per hour and lasted thirty hours, it lashed the Lower Keys, where the men were working. It was as if hurricanes were following them down the islands to wreak havoc on the railroad. The storm made channels out of roadbeds and washed out nearly 600 feet of track. It displaced the center span of the Bahia Honda Bridge, the foundation of which had consumed a freighter of sand, gravel, and concrete. Still, only three men died.

By then Flagler was eighty-two, nearly blind, and physically frail, and he knew he didn't have long to live. As if Krome didn't have enough to worry about, Flagler's underlings kept after him to finish the railroad so their boss could make the first journey all the way to Key West. Near the end of February 1911 one of them demanded that Krome finish by January 2, 1912, Flagler's birthday. That was a year early. "I did some close figuring," Krome wrote, "and finally replied that we could complete the road by January 22 of that year should no storm overtake us, or no unforeseen delay set us back."

He started building the track from both ends, with several teams working out of Key West and others completing the job from Knight's Key, south and west. The work went on twenty-four hours a day, seven days a week. From Key West to Stock Island the men poured and shoveled fill, then laid track.

On Key West the men built a terminal and a permanent pier, 1,700 feet long and 134 feet wide, so trains could load and unload and passenger ships could dock, allowing train riders to walk just a few feet from train to ship or ship to train.

The crews finished one day ahead of schedule, on January 21, 1912. That afternoon a pilot crew boarded a train, crossed the bridge, and chugged into Key West for the first unofficial time. Early the next morning the Overseas Extension Special departed Miami towing five cars, including Number 90, with Flagler himself on board. The entire train was packed to the gills with Florida East Coast Railway officials, and Flagler's car contained political bigwigs and diplomats from Latin America. No worker who had actually built the roadbed or laid a foot of railroad track was on board.

The Railway's opening began a three-day celebration in Key West. When the train rolled in, ships in the harbor blew their whistles while schoolchildren tossed flowers at Flagler's feet. The mayor gave a speech and the band played; a crowd of some 10,000 turned up, most of whom had never seen a train.

The Overseas Railway had cost $27 million and about 300 lives. Sixteen months later Henry Morrison Flagler died.

—⊗⊗⊗—

At first nearly everything went according to Flagler's plan. The railroad transported cargoes, including fresh pineapples from Cuba and limes, oranges, grapefruits, and sponges from the Keys. But the project never came close to paying for itself. After an initial surge of riders enthused by the notion of locomoting across the open sea, ridership tailed off in the 1920s as Americans were seduced by the automobile. Then the Great Depression hit, and instead of taking folks to Key West, the railroad carried natives away. The town's population sank from 22,000 to 12,500. Broke, the Railway went into receivership. Key West, once the nation's richest city per capita, declared bankruptcy in 1934, throwing itself on the mercy of the state, which pleaded with the federal government for help.

To solve Key West's problems, the Roosevelt Administration turned to Julius Stone, administrator of Florida's Emergency Relief Administration. Stone, an ambitious man, had earlier run New York State's welfare program under then-Governor Roosevelt. He would later claim that he'd steered Key West into his domain by prompting Governor David Sholtz's decision to place the town under FERA jurisdiction. Armed with his new authority, Stone declared Key West the Gibraltar of the South, arguing that the city needed only a highway so that tourists could drive down, spend their money, and pump up the economy. Along the way they'd stop at the other Keys and pump up their economies, too. With tourists, Key West would reach solvency once again.

U.S. Highway 1, which ran along the state's eastern edge, was Florida's longest, heaviest-traveled route. Lined with palm trees transplanted from the Caribbean, mold-lined advertising signs for hotels and cabins, flashing neon signs for "Whiskey" and "Dance and Dine," roadside billboards for Burma-Shave, and dirty, hand-lettered evangelical signs that warned PREPARE TO MEET THY GOD, the highway met Flagler's railroad near Miami and stopped. From there, State Road 4A carried on in hopscotch fashion to Key West, but with a 35-mile uncompleted gap between Lower Matecumbe and No Name Keys. The U.S. Army Corps of Engineers estimated the cost of materials to extend the highway across that gap at $7.5 million, which the state and national governments managed to scrape together. The governments also pledged another $2.5 million for skilled labor: machine operators, bridge builders, boat operators. That would not leave much for unskilled labor—the men who would pave the road and build the bridge ramps.

Stone's plan—which may well have been embroidered by Louis Howe, FDR's principal political advisor—was genius, solving two problems at once. With FERA funds Stone would take veterans off FDR's hands and put them to work down in the Sunshine State. In late 1934 he asked his boss, Harry Hopkins, to send veterans—nearly 600 from all over the country—to Florida's Camp Foster, about 40 miles south of Jacksonville. There, the men stayed for two weeks of quarantine and conditioning—presumably to the climate, but perhaps also to alcohol withdrawal—then they rode down to the end of the road at Lower Matecumbe Key to build a road and a bridge.

Hopkins also arranged for 143 veterans living in Washington, D.C., to head down to Camp Foster. "Give a man a dole and you save his body and destroy his spirit," Hopkins said. "Give him a job and pay him an assured wage, and you save both the body and the spirit." That he could, at the same time, remove a problem from Washington only made the politics more elegant.

Frenchy Fecteau, who by this time had served nearly three tours in the CCC, heard of these veterans' camps "where I could better myself"—that is, keep earning money—so he put in his application. Accepted in February 1935, he left his wife and children in Washington and chugged south in his Chevy pickup from the cold North to Camp Foster. Frenchy stayed there for the requisite quarantine and conditioning, then received his transfer to Lower Matecumbe in late March. By late August of that year the veterans were settled in three camps in the Upper Keys. Camps 3 and 5 lay, respectively, on the southern and northern tips of Lower Matecumbe Key, three miles apart. Camp 1 was eight miles north of Camp 5 on Windley Key, a short distance below the road project quarry etched out of the keystone of Plantation Key.

Six other veterans with families joined Frenchy to form a camp unto themselves on Upper Matecumbe Key, between Camps 1 and 5. They included G. E. Robinson, director of Camp 5, and his family, and Benjamin Van Ness (who had once chauffeured an officer around France), his wife Laura, and their two daughters. The children liked playing on the narrow stretches of sand that passed for a beach. Frenchy looked forward to the time when his kids would be playing with them.

CHAPTER TWO

Friday
August 30, 1935
Turks and Caicos Islands

*O*n Friday morning, as Frenchy Fecteau pocketed his $36
from the federal government, a tropical disturbance was
born just northeast of the Turks and Caicos Islands, eight tiny
lumps of treeless sand lying more than 600 miles southeast of
Miami and 700 miles east and a bit south of Havana. The Turks
and Caicos were a strange place for the storm's birth. Most
begin nearer the equator, between Africa and South America,
where the sun's direct rays heat the tropical Atlantic's surface
layers. The Turks and Caicos lie north of Hispaniola, between
the Tropic of Cancer and the twentieth parallel, almost too far
north for a storm in the making. But it was an excellent place
for a disturbance to develop undetected in 1935. Just over 5,000

people scraped a living from the sea surrounding those spots of sand, and only a few ships steamed past. The nearest weather observation stations were in the Caribbean and Cuba, at least 200 miles away.

The developing storm was a blind force, devoid of sympathy, malice, or any knowledge of its origins or destiny. It was merely a temporary cog in a planetary engine, an ad hoc mechanism for transporting heat from the tropics to the temperate latitudes. Yet, like a living thing, it was born, and it would grow, mature, decay, and die. In its prime it would be powerful, deadly, even beautiful when viewed from afar. People would call it angry, malevolent, evil, pitiless—but those people would be trying to make sense out of otherwise meaningless destruction. Some of them would be trying to blame the storm for things they should have done, but didn't.

Like all tropical disturbances, this one was sparked to life by the ocean's heat. By late August the sun had been beating down upon those seas at full force for four months, warming the water from the surface down to 200 feet from about 80 to 86 degrees Fahrenheit, a comfortable temperature for swimming. That deep lens of heated water evaporated readily into the air overhead, and when the warm, moist air rose, its vapor condensed into clouds and rain, releasing the heat that had been absorbed by evaporation. This kept the air relatively warm and buoyant, and soon cumulonimbus clouds climbed from the surface to the stratosphere. Dry air rushed in to replace the rising moist air, then picked up moisture and continued the cycle. The warm ocean was the engine, water vapor the fuel, and a system of thunderstorms and squalls the result.

And there it might have ended, as most thunderstorms over tropical seas do, the storm cell drowning in its own cold rain. But this one didn't. Somehow it developed the slightly lower air pressure and closed circulation that would have earned it the label of "tropical depression" from hurricane forecasters seventy years later. In 1935, the Weather Bureau used the term "tropical disturbance" to describe a system with twenty-four or more hours of organized convection and a diameter of 100 to 300 nautical miles.

On rare occasions a tropical disturbance grows into a hurricane. As air converges into the nascent storm, the Coriolis force—the counterclockwise deflection of northern hemisphere winds caused by the Earth's rotation—diverts it to the right. The spiraling storm creates a warm, clear eye, a calm center surrounded by a wall of high-speed wind. From miles above the storm it resembles the Milky Way galaxy swirling placidly over the ocean. Moisture-laden air continues to rise, pulling heat from the sea and casting it forth aloft to stoke the wind even more. At around 50,000 feet the rising air rushes away from the center, its vapor condensing and forming thunderstorms that blacken the sky and erupt with jagged flashes of lightning. Once that starts, the main concern of people in its predicted path becomes the speed of the wind circling the eye.

Today, when the wind speed in a tropical depression reaches 34 knots, or 39 miles per hour, meteorologists call it a tropical storm; when it reaches 74 miles per hour they declare it a hurricane. At full blast a hurricane expends more than enough energy to power all the dams, steam power plants, trains, and ships in the world. At full blast a hurricane roars like a freight train rocketing by at top speed, inches from where you stand.

The first European to survive such force was none other than Christopher Columbus. On his second voyage to the New World, in 1495, a more powerful storm than any "civilized" man had ever experienced sank two of his three galleons. The Spaniards adopted the Mayan name for these fierce storms, *Hunraken*, after the ancient wind god. In the Pacific Ocean the Chinese christened them "typhoons," for "great wind." In the Indian Ocean they were known as a "cyclones," after the Greek *kykloma*, meaning "wheel." All three words stood for the same thing: a huge, circular tropical storm of violent proportions.

Not all hurricanes blow equally. Scientists have long known this, but in 1969 the World Meteorological Organization published a paper addressing the topic. Dr. Robert Simpson, director of the National Hurricane Center, and Herbert Saffir, a consulting engineer, delineated what would become known as the Saffir-Simpson scale. Saffir concocted the structural damage scale, while Dr. Simpson devised the storm surge scale—the height of the dome of water lifted by a hurricane's lower air pressure. In Saffir-Simpson terms, the weakest hurricane is a Category 1, in which the winds register between 74 and 95 miles per hour and the storm surge is 4 to 5 feet high. A Category 1 storm inflicts minor damage to trees, piers, and low roads. Category 2 blows a bit stronger; the winds climb to 110 miles per hour and the surge reaches from 6 to 8 feet. Trees topple and marinas and coastal roads flood in a Category 2, and people should evacuate low-lying areas. In Category 3, the winds spin up to 130 miles per hour, while the surge is 9 to 12 feet high. Large trees topple. So do utility poles. Mobile homes fly away, and debris pounds coastal structures. In Category 4, the winds reach 131 to 155 miles per hour, and the surge reaches as high as 18 feet. A storm like that destroys roofs, doors, and windows and causes major erosion. The beach and foreshore wash away, and all people within two miles of shore must evacuate or risk drowning.

But the worst is Category 5. The winds blow with a force greater than 155 miles per hour, while the storm surge climbs higher than 18 feet—taller than three men standing on one another's shoulders. Solid buildings tumble, their windows and doors blown out. Outside it becomes impossible to stand. If you could stand—or if the wind kept you lying in an exposed location—the sand would blast your skin raw, and might even tear flesh from bone. Category 5 hurricanes are rare. During the twentieth century just three struck the United States.

The most recent, Andrew, hit Homestead, Florida, early on August 24, 1992, a Monday. With winds gusting to 175 miles per hour, a storm surge of 19 to 23 feet, and atmospheric pressure dropping to 27.23 inches of mercury—the recognized average air pressure worldwide is 29.92—the hurricane destroyed 25,524 homes and damaged 101,241 more; it wiped out 99 percent of all mobile homes. Some 300,000 people were rendered homeless, and the hurricane caused a record $30 billion in damage. Yet only twenty-six people died.

While Andrew destroyed more property than any other hurricane, Hurricane Camille was a larger storm—at least in its area of destruction. It hit the mainland on Sunday, August 17, 1969—a weekend when the nation was focused on a festival of peace and love in Woodstock, New York. Reaching a wind speed of 160 miles per hour and an air pressure drop to 26.72, Camille raised a record storm surge of more than 22 feet when it made landfall at Bay St. Louis, Mississippi. While local officials managed to evacuate 81,000 of the 150,000 residents in the storm zone, 172 people still died as the hurricane carved a path through Mississippi, Tennessee, Kentucky, and Virginia. It destroyed 5,400 homes and damaged 12,500 more, many of those in mudslides.

The third Category 5 hurricane was America's most violent storm of the twentieth century.

⸎

Before the National Weather Service existed, people got their predictions from the U.S. Weather Bureau, established just four years after the end of the Civil War, when President Ulysses S. Grant ordered the U.S. Signal Corps to record weather observations at all military posts across the country. The government converted the Bureau into a civilian agency in 1891 and transferred it to the Department of Agriculture. By 1935 the Weather Bureau collected data twice a day—at 8:00 A.M. and 8:00 P.M., Greenwich Mean Time—at stations across the forty-eight states and Mexico, Central America, the West Indies, the Bahamas, and Cuba.

Until that year all hurricane predictions came directly from Weather Bureau headquarters in Washington, D.C. But in 1933 a record twenty-one tropical storms spun up, nine of them exploding into full-fledged hurricanes. One year later a hurricane whirled out of nowhere and brushed against Galveston, Texas. The storm wasn't especially destructive, but it caught the full attention of a city that had been blasted with little warning by an extremely powerful hurricane at the turn of the century, killing 6,000 people. That was the greatest loss of life from a natural disaster in U.S. history.

Given all the tropical storms in the first two years of his administration, FDR deemed the centralized system too sluggish and clumsy, and split it into smaller offices nearer to storm-prone areas. Stations were opened in Boston; New Orleans; San Juan, Puerto Rico; and Jacksonville, Florida. Located on the fifth floor of the Post Office Building, a one-block-square Art Deco stone building built by Roosevelt's WPA, the Jacksonville office issued its first report in early July 1935 while still four men short of a full staff.

Back then the Weather Bureau issued storm information under three different levels of severity. The lowest, called an "advisory" (or an "advice," as the Bureau sometimes quaintly put it), consisted of little more than a storm's location, intensity, and direction. The Bureau issued an advisory when a storm lacked much power and stood well away from the coastline. The next step up was a "storm warning," which likewise included the location, intensity, and direction of the storm, but also indicated that people close to the warning area might receive strong winds. The third level, a "hurricane warning," meant that the storm had reached hurricane speeds.

Along with its small reporting stations on the U.S. coast—often just a single observer operating with a barometer, an anemometer, and little else—the Weather Bureau received regular reports from Coast Guard stations and from Pan American Airways, which flew routes from Florida to South America. During the heat of summer in areas known to breed tropical storms—the Caribbean, the Gulf of Mexico, and the Atlantic Ocean—the Bureau received supplemental reports every six hours from ships at sea and from weather stations along the Gulf Coast and south of Jacksonville, Florida, at midnight, 6:00 A.M., 12:00 P.M., and 6:00 P.M., GMT. It took time to compile the information and to interpret, chart, and disseminate it—typically two hours. Once the Jacksonville office finished a report, radio stations WIOD and WQAM would broadcast it directly from the office, and the Bureau sent copies by teletype to all the local newspapers and news agencies, such as the Associated Press. Ordinary people could even phone in and receive the most recent report.

Of course, not everyone relied on the Weather Bureau. Those who made their living from the sea or who simply didn't have a telephone might forecast the weather with an experienced eye and a barometer. They also kept watch on lighthouses and shore stations. During the day, a red triangular pennant flying above a square red flag with a black square in the center signaled an approaching storm. And at night two red lanterns mounted one on top of the other signaled the same thing. For hurricanes, the signal was two black-centered red flags in daytime and two red lanterns with a white one in between at night. A hurricane warning meant "an immediate need of precautionary measures to save life and property."

—⟨⟨⟨⟩⟩⟩—

The tradition of naming tropical storms didn't begin until World War II, when meteorologists in the U.S. Army, Air Force, and Navy started naming them after their wives and girlfriends, or women they wanted as their wives or girlfriends, or women who had dumped them. In 1950 someone got the idea of naming Atlantic hurricanes from the military phonetic alphabet, such as Hurricane Able, Hurricane Baker, Hurricane Charlie, and so on. That lasted until 1953, when the Weather Bureau first released an annual list that retained an alphabetic sequence while returning to women's names. A hurricane hath more fury than a woman scorned, someone must have figured. And so, in 1953, Hurricane Florence blew through, and in 1956, Hurricane Flossy. In 1979, amidst the general drive for equal rights, the World Meteorological Organization decreed that the annual list would alternate male and female names and that the names could be recycled every six years unless a storm was particularly noteworthy for its destruction. Thus, Hurricane Alex may reappear, but there will be no future Andrews or Camilles.

Prior to World War II, hurricanes derived names only on the basis of association—the place or the date they made landfall, for example.

The first word of a tropical disturbance on Friday, August 30, 1935, came from the Jacksonville office at 9:30 P.M. in the form of a standard weather bulletin:

> Conditions remain unsettled and slightly squally east of
> the Bahamas and north of Turk Island, with evidence
> of a weak circulation but no strong winds. This seems to
> be working northwestward or northward.

No one could foresee that this weak disturbance would become America's first and most powerful Category 5 storm of the twentieth century. The National Weather Service would call it the 1935 Labor Day Hurricane, but in the Keys it would still be remembered seventy years later as, simply, the Great Hurricane.

CHAPTER THREE

Saturday
August 31, 1935
Florida Keys

By late Saturday morning the work camps were notice-
ably quieter. The previous day, 683 other veterans had
joined Frenchy Fecteau in picking up their paychecks, and
within hours, according to the Monroe County deputy sheriff who accompanied the paymaster, many were drunk. Since
then, however, almost 300 of them had disappeared for the
long Labor Day weekend. The All Stars Veterans baseball
team—with Ben Davis, superintendent of Camp 3, playing
catcher—had driven off in stake-bed Chevy trucks for a Sunday game against the team from the relief camp at Ojus,
north of Miami. More than 100 veterans had followed them
there in more stake-bed Chevys to show their support and

to continue drinking, in no particular order. A few men went fishing, several of them getting paid by rich folks staying down at Long Key Fishing Camp to guide them to where the kingfish were biting. Some headed for Key West and a weekend of carousing. Eleven men stole a truck and set out for Washington to visit the president, or at least that was their stated plan.

But the cooks, the medical corps, and the officials' drivers were required to stay on duty throughout the long weekend. For them the holiday was just another workday. And many of the ordinary laborers were staying as well, either to save money, like Frenchy, or because other options lacked appeal. All told, as many as 400 men were sticking around the camps.

The local weather was supposed to be nice. The Friday edition of the *Key West Citizen* had predicted a Friday high of 90 degrees and a low of 81, offering a forecast of "partly cloudy tonight and Saturday with local showers Saturday, gentle to moderate winds Sunday, winds becoming variable." The men staying in the camps assumed they could look forward to a reasonably comfortable weekend.

Not too many months before, the men would have trampled each other to get away for a weekend. Life in the camps from their inception in late 1934 through early 1935 almost lived up to the Spanish phrase for the Keys they occupied, *mate hombre*—"kill man."

The first veterans shipped down to the tropical Upper Keys by the Federal Emergency Relief Administration disembarked from the train in November 1934 and immediately began building two camps. At Windley Key, about two miles north of the village of Islamorada on Upper Matecumbe Key and just below the quarry on Plantation Key, they clear-cut an area of brush on the Atlantic side for Camp 1 and pitched Army tents just like the ones they'd lived in during the war. Eleven miles south, on the lower end of Lower Matecumbe Key—at least a two-hour walk away—other vets, working with skilled civilians, scraped clean the ferry landing already there and cleared the ground for Camp 3 so they could build a bridge to span the ocean south to Jewfish Key. The bridge would be three and a half miles long. Both camps faced the Atlantic for whatever relief from the heat and mosquitoes the ocean breezes could offer.

"If the U.S. had a Devil's Island, the Florida Keys would be a good place to locate it," *Time* magazine reported. It wasn't the weather—not in winter, at least, when the veterans first arrived. Average daytime temperatures were topping out at 65 to 75 degrees, dropping to a comfortable 55 or so at night. But the weather in those early months was about the only positive.

According to Albert C. Keith, later the editor of the weekly *Key Veteran News* but at the time just another vet, FERA officials promised the veterans civilian clothes and even took their measurements, but that was as close as the men came to getting them. The vets bunked down in Camp 1 before it had bathing facilities. "I do know the sanitary conditions of the camp were almost beyond . . . well, I couldn't understand," Keith said. Flies were thick and infested the food. No fresh-water source existed on the Keys, so the government hauled water down from the mainland in tank cars for the men, and for a time they barely had enough to drink. Forced to bathe in seawater, they couldn't get their soap to lather. They had no lumber to build more permanent shelters, and they even ran short of the old Army tents. They resorted to pitching circus tents. "That was December, after the hurricane season," said thirty-three-year-old Hubert Campbell Nichols of mainland Homestead, who worked as a civil engineer on the road project. At least they wouldn't blow away.

Low mangrove swamps wrapped the shores, each tree with hundreds of gnarled roots that snagged floating debris: seaweed, wood, soda and liquor bottles, cork stoppers, and trash. That's why Conchs called mangroves "island builders." Offshore from the narrow islands lay nothing but the reef and the sea, with barracuda and poisonous stingrays swimming about. And sharks. One of the camps had a fine piano player whose last name was Lemon—the veterans seldom knew anyone by more than a nickname or last name. One day Lemon said, "I think I'll have a swim before lunch," and was never seen again. Someone found his clothes, and everyone combed the area for a couple of days, but he never turned up. The sharks got him, they figured.

Chopping down the thick brush, the vets found rattlesnakes. And then there were the bugs. "The mosquitoes were serious," wrote one old soldier, Robert Traynor, years later. "They would attack in heavy black swarms, and their happy hum couldn't be missed. They were like miniature bee swarms—only more vicious and demanding. It took a man with a cabbage tree frond mosquito brush . . . constantly beating the mosquitoes off of all the workers, or otherwise the inflicted pain would have been too severe. If the worker and the beater stopped for even a second, these insects would settle on the worker's blue denim jumpers, and they went from blue to black. And then if someone ran both hands down the worker's back and turned his hands over, they looked as if they had been dipped in a pan of blood."

Thankfully, the winter months marked the seasonal low for the mosquito population as well as temperatures. There would be worse to come. Indeed, mosquitoes had been a principal factor in limiting the entire population of the Keys outside Key West to not much more than 1,000 people.

FERA administrator Captain G. E. Robinson supervised the camps, but their construction, and the men's work in general, was overseen by state highway department engineers. Neither Robinson nor the roadwork supervisors, B. M. Duncan and Lawrence Bow, had much regard for the men's work habits, and the divided command took its toll. Few precautions were taken concerning the men's safety. The camps held no fire drills, and no hurricane drills, for that matter. A few churchgoers attended the Methodist church in Islamorada, but the closest priest was Father McDonald up in Homestead. The veterans had neither books to read nor movies to watch. They were promised a recreation hall at Camp 1, but promises were all they received. As for the food, like their tents, it also seemed to date back to World War I. "I had considerable trouble in getting satisfactory cooperation from the officials concerning the balanced diets to be made up in the mess hall," said Harry Smith, mess sergeant for Camp 3. "I was forced to take what rations were given me." As more and more veterans arrived from the North, the two crowded camps grew so filthy with human waste that two vets died from spinal meningitis.

Conditions deteriorated to the point that Camp 3 vets formed a five-man grievance committee in February. The camp administration arrested and jailed the five without charges, so the men of the camp went on strike. Monroe County Sheriff Karl Thompson called on Governor David Sholtz to send in the National Guard. But when the press followed and filed stories, the government capitulated, called off the troops, and cleaned up the camps, with FERA assuming undivided responsibility for the men's welfare.

Camp administrators started providing truck rides north to the outdoor movie theater at Tavernier, which had electricity from a small generating plant. (Upper Matecumbe, too, had two small electrical plants, and there was one in Camp 3.) The Homestead library sent down books and magazines. Construction on the recreation hall started that summer, and administrators replaced the tents with four-man huts— "shacks," as the vets called them. Each measured approximately 20 by 10 feet, with walls built from one-by-six planks to a height of 2 feet, just above the beds, with mosquito netting above that. The roof consisted of tarpaper on wood, or sometimes just canvas. These shacks sat on wooden pilings or concrete blocks, but if they lay above keystone outcroppings, they might be bolted down. The ones that weren't anchored had sand piled up around them to hold them in place.

Each camp held sixty or more of these shacks, laid out in neat rows. To house even more veterans, FERA built another camp, Camp 5, at the north end of Lower Matecumbe Key. That camp was low to the water—sometimes the tide rolled up to the kitchen floor and put the cooking fires out, according to Frenchy—but there were also fewer mosquitoes. The nearby Matecumbe Hotel became the Administrative Building for all three camps, with second-floor offices and living quarters for thirty-five staff. The arrangement brought welcome security in a lean time to hotel owner Ed Butters and his wife, Fern.

Due partly to the strike, partly to rapid promotion, and partly to the unpleasant aspects of babysitting camps of crude, loud, belligerent veterans, none of the camp leaders stayed around long. "They changed so often that before you got acquainted with one fellow, another was in charge," explained John A. Russell, postmaster of Islamorada on Upper Matecumbe Key. "Mr. Henchman [William H.D. Hinchman, previously FERA's assistant regional engineer for the Southeast] came first [March 18], and when we got acquainted with him, they moved him and then [April 1] Mr. Ghent came.

When he got acquainted, he left Jack Little in charge. When Jack Little left, they sent Mr. Sheldon." But the National Guard remained until May 13, when FERA officials concluded that the vets no longer presented a problem. Yet the vets' crude behavior, their drinking and fighting and profanity, continued to scandalize passengers aboard trains heading to and from Key West.

———— ∞∞∞ ————

For nearly three months after Frenchy Fecteau arrived in February, the mosquitoes tried to eat him alive. By May the mosquitoes were oppressive enough to drive the men into their shacks from dusk to morning, sometimes turning their lights out at night so as not to attract more. With all his piloting skills and urges to better himself, Frenchy was assigned to be a spraying engineer, which meant manning one of the small cylinders that sprayed creosote and crankcase oil on the mosquitoes. Like all the other relief jobs, it paid $30 a month. The toxic mix killed mosquito eggs, all right, but it kept blowing back into his eyes and nearly blinded him.

Dr. Main—again, no one seemed to recall his first name— at the Snake Creek Hospital near Camp 1 took care of him, and when he discharged Fecteau, Dr. Main told camp administrators that Frenchy needed a different job. They made him assistant timekeeper, a job that had recently been created to keep the vets honest; otherwise, some of them wouldn't have shown up for work. Five days a week, the timekeeper for each camp logged the men in for the morning shift and once again for the afternoon shift. If the men didn't work, they didn't get paid. Those who weren't fit enough for roadwork were assigned lighter duty, like working in the mess. Frenchy wrote attendance down in the monthly paybooks. He was not unhappy about his new job. It not only kept the creosote out of his eyes, but earned him an extra $6 a month. And the time he wasn't out in the camps, he worked inside the Administrative Building, otherwise known as Headquarters.

Once the veterans had protested, gotten the mosquitoes under control, obtained enough water to drink and bathe in from a continual series of railroad tank cars towed down from the mainland and parked along a siding, and bunked down in their new shacks, the camps felt a little more pleasant. Still, it was hot and humid, especially in the summer. Daytime highs routinely made it above 90 degrees, and overnight lows hovered in the upper seventies. With the average daily humidity above 80 percent, a man's shirt would soak with sweat in minutes, and hot rain poured down at least once a day. But at least on the Atlantic side there was usually a breeze off the sea, and as the locals say everywhere, "If you don't like the weather, just wait five minutes and it'll change." In the Florida Keys that was the truth. Sunny and hot, followed by a thunderstorm, then sunny, hot, and muggy.

Upper Matecumbe Key was four miles long and narrow, not more than 300 feet wide. Standing in its center, the men could have seen the Atlantic to the east and Florida Bay and the Gulf of Mexico to the west were it not for the thick brush that obscured the view. The Key's only distinguishing features were the railroad tracks down its center, the new highway paralleling the tracks, and the small community of Islamorada.

Lower Matecumbe was a different story. It had a bit of a sandy beach and coconut trees. Except for the "skeeters," some of the men said, living there was like a year-round vacation—or at least that's what FERA officials claimed the men said. "I would say that the men were not only contented, but the word got around that it was a good place to be, and we had more people wanting to go there than we could send," Julius Stone said. Of course Stone *would* say that—he wanted the overseas highway built to turn Key West into a tourist mecca.

After the strike the food did get better and everybody got their fill. For breakfast the men ate fried eggs, fried potatoes, cereal, coffee, and condensed milk. Real milk wouldn't keep in the heat. At dinner they had roast beef, roast pork, or roast lamb, all the salad they could eat, and all the limeade they could drink, thanks to Key limes.

The food might have been a little too good, according to the *Miami Daily News*. One Sunday the newspaper's feature reporter stopped by for lunch and wrote that the camp cooks served turkey. He thought turkey a little plush. Other reporters wrote about the camps' seamier side, saying that the men drank and fought continuously and ultimately seemed like nothing but trouble. "About half were psychopaths. Most of their pay went to liquor dealers and moonshines," one reporter wrote in *Time* magazine. Right after the men were paid and during holidays, the camp doctors experienced what they called "boom days," when they'd perform extra duty suturing veterans' wounds. Still, the writer added, "More nuisance than menace . . . the veterans were so broken-spirited that [a] two-man police force could handle any number of them with the greatest of ease." A *New York Times* reporter divided the workers into three types: "Shell-shocked, whiskey-shocked, depression-shocked."

Indeed, drinking was a problem. Until Ray Sheldon took over the three camps on August 1, 1935, the men received $1 three times a week as an advance on their monthly wages. With beer a dime a bottle at the canteen, they could stay drunk all week long. Sheldon changed the allowance policy so that every man received a $2 advance each Friday. "That cut down the drinking considerably and at the same time boosted the deposits in the Trust Fund," said Frederick Poock, sixty-two-year-old camp paymaster and unofficial savings officer. "Of course they drank on payday just the same."

Yet many were sober, hardworking family men who had simply fallen on hard times. Willis Evers, a forty-year-old camp cook for the civilians who ran the heavy machinery on the bridge project, said, "As I knew the veterans, the ones that worked with me were very conscientious and obedient, and I thoroughly believed the average ones meant the best."

The main work project consisted of building the overseas highway, which ran alongside the Overseas Railway. Huge power saws cut big slabs of beautiful keystone from the quarry on Plantation Key, but it was still tough work—keystone seemed nearly as hard as diamonds. The men would pound the slabs into submission with sledgehammers—"making little ones out of big ones," they called it—then shovel the gravel onto one of the big Chevrolet stake-bed trucks and haul it to the end of the road at the southern extremity of Lower Matecumbe Key. There other vets shoveled the gravel onto the road, and still others tamped it down with hand rollers. Once it was smooth and level, more vets swept on a layer of hot tar with blackened push brooms, or sometimes left it bare. While all this was going on, other workers built or improved picnic and parking areas where travelers could stop their cars and take in the glory of the Keys over a packed lunch.

According to *Saturday Evening Post* writer Marjory Stoneman Douglas, however, between January and August they managed to lengthen the highway just 200 feet. She concluded that the road was a make-work project for bums who didn't want to work. But in fact, like all of the Roosevelt make-work projects, the highway was designed to be heavy on manpower and light on the cost of materials. The objective was to get money into people's pockets. Making breakneck progress, rocketing along like Flagler's railroad crews around the turn of the century, was not the point.

The more skilled workers among the veterans were as-signed more complex projects than spreading gravel. East of Islamorada sat the Matecumbe Methodist Church, with its rotting foundation and swayback floors. The church had been built on a nearby island in 1884 and transported to Upper Matecumbe by raft six years later. It rested on the beach just north of Pioneer Cemetery, where a four-foot-tall marble angel stood vigil over the grave of Etta Delores Pin-der: born July 15, 1899; died February 21, 1914. For decades the Conchs had been bringing their ragged children to the one-room school building next to the church for the educa-tion they themselves had never had. Since the start of the Great Depression, enrollment had grown to the point that the students now overflowed the front door and into the churchyard. The government allocated funding for a new school that would double as a hurricane shelter. The veter-ans sawed keystone blocks and began building it. In Ta-vernier they began work on a concrete movie theater next door to the existing outdoor theater.

The south end of Lower Matecumbe Key needed an au-tomobile bridge to connect it to Jewfish Key (later renamed Fiesta Key) just off the northeast end of Long Key. This long span would bypass Craig Key, making the route a few thou-sand feet shorter than the railroad. A crew of civilians and vets were assigned to build the ramps leading up to and away from the bridge and to set up cofferdams between the Keys. Meanwhile, the crews manned steam derricks, dredge boats, caterpillar cranes, and pumps.

Colonel Ed Sheeran led them. He didn't care much for the vets assigned to him to help clear-cut brush and perform other low-skill duties; in his opinion they weren't very good help. "There were some who never worked and who never will," he said.

Now sixty-five, Sheeran had helped build Flagler's Overseas Railway a quarter century earlier, and in fact had led a work crew through the hurricanes of 1909 and 1910. He took a great deal of pride that while more than 125 died in the '06 hurricane, fewer than fifteen men under him died in the '09 hurricane—they drowned when their oceangoing tug broke apart and sank—and his crew suffered just one death in the 1910 storm. Colonel Sheeran himself was a veteran. He'd been a combat engineer in the Great War, though nearly fifty years old at the time, and had reached the rank of major. Wounded while working on a bridge under German fire, he'd earned a Purple Heart and a citation for bravery. Keys residents unofficially promoted him to colonel.

Sheeran's civilian crew put in forty or more hours a week and sometimes worked six or seven days, but the veterans worked no more than thirty hours and five days a week. They started later than the civilians, took off early for a two-hour lunch, and got off early for the day. The rest of their time they would often spend drinking, fighting, and loafing—not the kind of lifestyle that won Colonel Sheeran's approval.

Of course, the veterans did other things in their free time. Some liked to fish, or spear what was called Florida lobster, which weren't actually lobsters but big crawfish. The veterans thought they were delicious—at least better than down-and-out Depression fare like dough fried in bacon grease or the grub served in the mess halls. Each crawfish weighed five or six pounds. They caught them at night from a flat-bottom rowboat, and the camps' cooks would let them borrow a big pot to boil the crawfish if the veterans returned the pot scrubbed clean.

On weekends the men could sign out a truck from the camps and drive into Miami, or take the Overseas Railway into Key West, where the cops took it easy on them when they started drinking and fighting. Ernest Hemingway himself often bent elbows with them at a local bar like Sloppy Joe's, swapping war stories. Best of all was a two-story bordello built of bare board pine shingles. Alice Reed owned it, and many of the vets headed straight there when they reached town.

⸺

On Saturday morning, August 31, Ray Sheldon sat in his second-story office in the Administrative Building and dealt another hand of poker to a couple of the other administrators: his assistant, Sam Cutler, and William "Bill" Hardaker, director of Camp 1. Sheldon's mind was less on the game and even less on the veterans, and more on the new Mrs. Sheldon, Gayle Colvert, from Miami. They had married in a hurry in Miami on the last day of July, right after Fred Ghent, director of the veterans' work camps throughout Florida, had told Sheldon to report to Matecumbe Key. The marriage was Sheldon's second; his first wife had died the previous year. Finally, after a month of getting himself settled in the camps, Sheldon made reservations at the La Concha Hotel in Key West for a two-day honeymoon. The ferry would leave at one-thirty that afternoon, and he wanted to be on board.

The only potential obstacle to that plan arose late in the morning. Colonel Sheeran testified later that he had gone to the hotel and demanded to see Sheldon. Sheldon put down his cards, stepped outside his office, and walked down the stairs to see him. The colonel told Sheldon that he'd read about a hurricane 800 miles away and had overheard the Conchs saying that a storm was coming, and that in fact the Conchs had started boarding up their shacks. The hurricane was going to hit Matecumbe Key, the colonel said, and he told Sheldon that he needed to order the emergency relief train. But the barometer read near 30 inches, and Sheldon dismissed the colonel's fears, merely assuring Sheeran that he'd keep an eye on every barometer he saw while he was in Key West. Then he bade Colonel Sheeran good-bye and walked back upstairs.

Early that afternoon, after a few more hands of poker, Sheldon and his wife Gayle got into their car and drove down to the ferry dock at Camp 3. They could have taken the train to Key West, but riding the ferry would give them the use of their car while there. Despite orders posted to the camp bulletin board ("If any leaders leave, leave a responsible person in their place"), Sheldon left no one in charge of the three camps; instead he told each camp leader that he could be reached by phone in Key West. But Sam Cutler, his fifty-nine-year-old second-in-command, had worked nearly every weekend that summer, so he moved into Sheldon's office. Sheldon drove the car on board Captain Charles Albury's one-thirty ferry for the four-hour ride to No Name Key, which would be followed by the 45-mile drive from there to Key West. Under steam finally, the newlyweds, looking over the rail, noticed something unusual: tarpon were swimming west through the Keys, from the Atlantic side to the Florida Bay side "in droves and herds, flocks and schools, by the thousands," according to a fisherman who witnessed it. "[Tarpon] always do [it] in a heavy hurricane season."

On board Albury's ferry, the *Monroe County*, the barometer read 29.90, gradually rising. "You cannot depend on the markings of a barometer," Sheldon would say in a deposition taken later; he knew that readings could vary as much as 0.12 inch of mercury on a nice, clear day. When readings plunge to 29.50, conditions outside can get pretty hairy, but a rising barometer like the one on the ferry suggested to him that things would be just fine.

They were on their honeymoon at last.

—◦◦◦—

Forty-five years old, Sheldon had worked in the construction business for some time—twenty to twenty-five years, he said. A Massachusetts native, he had moved to Florida in the 1920s and had held down a job throughout the Depression. After voters swept FDR into office, Sheldon took a job as an inspector with the Public Works Administration in Palm Beach County. But FDR eliminated the PWA in early 1935—its projects took too long from conception to the beginning of construction, cost too much, and employed too few men—replacing it with the WPA. When Sheldon transferred to FERA, he first became director of operations for Valusia, Hope, Flagler, and Lake counties. Then he went down to head up the camps on Matecumbe Key.

While no one questioned his skills as a construction engineering boss, after only one month in charge some found Sheldon arrogant and dictatorial. "My honest opinion," said Wilbur Jones, assistant to the camp auditor, "is that I thought Mr. Sheldon was the type that wouldn't listen to anybody else, and would do what he wanted to, and what I could say would have no effect. And therefore, I would probably be better off if I just kept my opinion to myself." More agreed with Jones than not.

According to veteran John Good, the general storekeeper for all three camps:

Advising Mr. Sheldon wasn't an easy matter. In the first place [Sheldon had] what might be called second nature knowledge on every subject which could possibly be brought up in his presence. From the day he arrived at the veterans' camps . . . he attempted to leave the impression with all the members of the staff that they knew absolutely nothing concerning the camps that was unknown to him. Veterans' camps being a new thing, and my having been with those camps since their beginning, I felt—as did other members of the staff—that there were a great many things about which Mr. Sheldon should know, before giving definite orders about things which he knew nothing of. But I found that [giving] advice or constructive criticism was definitely out of order . . . It seemed that in every case when we men . . . made the proper suggestion to Mr. Sheldon, we were never allowed to finish . . . much less being asked for advice as to what orders should be given and how those orders should be carried out. Taken all in all Mr. Sheldon was very much out of place as acting head of the veterans' camps.

Good went on to list seven other staffers who felt the same way, from Sheldon's assistant, Sam Cutler, to the director of Camp 5, G. E. Robinson. Not everyone complained about him, however. "Blackie" Pugh, top sergeant of Camp 3, liked him. "I had confidence in the man, to be honest with you," he said. "The man had a responsible job and I felt like he was capable of handling it."

It was FERA administrator Ghent who had ordered Sheldon down to Matecumbe Key to take over the three veterans' camps. Born in Alabama, but a Florida resident since 1925, Ghent had served time in the Navy during World War I. Six weeks after the strike in February 1935, FERA tapped Ghent, previously director of safety for the Florida Emergency Relief Administration, to supervise all the veterans' camps in the state. (These included Camp 2 in St. Petersburg, Camp 4 in Clearwater, Camp 7 in Palatka, Camp 8 in Gainesville, and Camp 9 in Leesburg.) After spending several weeks at the work camps in the Keys, Ghent retreated to his statewide office in Jacksonville, where he was supplied a government car and a chauffeur to use as he saw fit. He never again stayed overnight in the Keys.

Ghent began his job as camp supervisor for all of Florida with good intentions, vowing to meet each man in each camp. W. N. Chambers, a vet assigned to Camp 3, did get an interview with him, and immediately asked Ghent what provisions he had made to get the men out in the event that a hurricane struck. After all, Chambers said, he'd lived through five of them himself, "and I had some knowledge of the damage that could be done, and especially in a place of that kind." Ghent promised Chambers that he had already arranged with the Florida Overseas Railway to have not one, but two trains—complete with cooking equipment in the baggage cars—there in the camps at the first sign of a hurricane.

But after just two days, Ghent abandoned his program to meet each man. "I was down there all the time that Ghent had the job, and I only saw the man twice," said Roy Hurley, who worked in the Snake Creek Hospital, a leased sporting lodge near Camp 1. One of those two times had to be in May 1935, when Ghent gave a speech, and afterward the men again asked what would happen to them if a storm hit. Again Ghent said not to worry; he'd arranged with the railroad to get a train there in five hours, and anyway, he knew of a storm's approach up to five days in advance. He had three barometers and a man posted at each, and if one gave a bad reading, they could always check it against the other two.

Conrad Van Hyning, the Tallahassee-based commissioner of the Emergency Relief Administration for the state of Florida, had been Ghent's boss only since July 1 but quickly formed a negative opinion of him. "I felt he was the nervous type and likely to jump at decisions," Van Hyning said later. By mid-August the veterans' work camps nationwide had endured several months of negative press coverage, with the *New York Times*, the *Washington Post*, and other newspapers decrying the inefficiencies in the program and the drunk and disorderly behavior of many of the vets. Support for the program waned in the Roosevelt Administration, and on August 16, Harry Hopkins announced that the work camps would close. On August 12, Van Hyning told Ghent that the bridge and road construction in the Keys would be transferred to the CCC in October, after which Ghent's services at FERA would no longer be required. The news came as a shock to Ghent.

⸎

At 1:00 P.M., shortly after Sheldon left the hotel, the Weather Bureau office in Jacksonville issued a second bulletin on the disturbance south of the Bahamas, its first since the previous evening. This time it was an advisory:

> Tropical disturbance of small diameter but considerable intensity central [centered] about sixty miles east of Long Island, Bahamas, apparently moving west northwestward, attended by strong shifting winds and probable gales near center. Caution advised southeastern Bahamas and ships in that vicinity. Further advices at 4:00 P.M.

That information was two hours old, and suggested that the system had traveled about 250 miles since the previous evening, or about 16 miles per hour. The developing storm was still a long way from land, but much closer than Colonel Sheeran had thought: about 440 statute miles away, and headed through the Straits of Florida.

The next advisory, which came out at three-thirty in the afternoon, instead of four o'clock as advertised, read:

> Tropical disturbance of small diameter central near Long Island, Bahamas, apparently moving west northwestward attended by fresh to strong shifting winds and squalls, possibly gale force near center. Caution advised Bahama Islands and ships in that vicinity.

The disturbance was still far from being a hurricane.

Seven weeks before the Labor Day weekend, the Upper Keys had received a glancing blow from a passing storm. Barometers aside, the Conchs could sense it coming. The signs were clear to them. The joints of elderly folks ached. Their mutts curled up nervously under the porches and refused to come out. Cats and chickens ran away to hide in the edges of the mangrove swamps. But it was the crabs that especially gave it away, migrating overland to the Gulf side like an army of skeletons crawling sideways from the Atlantic. Tarpon and other fish also evacuated the Atlantic for the Gulf. So while the Florida sky remained blue, the old Conchs sank their small boats in the inlets filled with trash and soda bottles and boarded up the windows of their bare wooden shacks that stood on stilts. Then they gathered up food and fresh water and crawled inside to wait out the coming storm.

From over the ocean the sky grew dark while lightning flashed on the horizon and thunder rumbled in the distance. The wind blew harder and harder, and the veterans could see the seas steepen and crest and hear the crashing on the beach. They saw the Conchs' shacks boarded up and ran to their own shacks, huddling there while the tide rose ankle deep, soaking the bare wooden floors with seawater. They climbed onto their mattresses, getting as high as they could, and waited in the dark.

But instead of the torrential rain the Conchs had predicted and the veterans expected, a mere patter fell on their roofs. By dawn the storm had blown over and the sun rose in a clear blue sky. Palm fronds, coconuts, shells, and garbage lay scattered across the low islands, alongside the railroad tracks. The storm, which had formed 800 miles southeast of Miami, continued to crawl due north until it struck Newfoundland a few days later.

Most of the veterans had never lived through a hurricane, had never even lived in a hurricane-prone region. They didn't know what one was. And most simply grew inured to the locals' warnings. "Ever since I have been down there, they have been talking about storms," said Ohio farmer French E. McClintic, of Camp 3. "It got so I didn't pay any attention to it at all." Others took a more manly posture. Louis Mahoney, the chief deputy sheriff, who lived in Key West, said, "The veterans themselves were not afraid of the hurricane and told me—lots of them—they didn't care about it coming—the hell with the hurricane—they had been through battles in France and let the hurricane come along."

After he arrived in the camps, Sheldon had made one quick improvement: He had the shacks cross-braced to withstand the wind. Van Hyning, noting that Sheldon had taken charge and shown initiative by improving the shacks, decided he would stay on the project under CCC oversight after October.

Saturday afternoon, while Sheldon and his wife were taking the ferry to Key West, forty-one-year-old Detroit veteran Tony Lapinski boarded the train to Key West with twelve others. When they pulled into Flagler Station, "All of the people were talking about the storm," he said. "They had their windows nailed up. Big apartment houses, big stores, and the ten-cent stores had their windows nailed up. The natives at Key West had prepared for the storm."

The Sheldons had trouble getting into town; Captain Albury's ferry broke down, and it took some time to repair. For a while they stretched their legs on the deck and watched the fish leaping and swimming toward the Gulf side of the Keys. The ride to No Name Key took even longer than usual. When they finally drove into Key West that evening, the Sheldons had a nice dinner, then made a detour before going to their hotel. "Mrs. Sheldon wished to purchase some postal cards," Sheldon said, "and while she was making her purchase I noticed from the Key West paper that the storm warnings were out." At 11:00 P.M. he called the Weather Bureau's Key West office on Front Street and spoke with meteorologist Gerald Kennedy, who told him that conditions around the Matacumbes "did not appear very alarming," but if anything changed he would call the hotel. Two hours later Sheldon finally fell asleep.

The veterans heard about the storm that day through their radios and by word of mouth. Those camp leaders still around for the Labor Day weekend told them the storm presented no threat. "[But] it looked kind of funny," Frenchy Fecteau remembered later, "because the truck drivers had orders to turn in their keys." They were never, ever, ordered to turn in their keys.

At nine-thirty that evening the Bureau sent out its last message for the day:

> The tropical disturbance is central tonight near or over the northern end of Long Island, Bahamas, moving rather slowly west northwestward, attended by strong shifting winds and squalls over a considerable area and probably gale force near center. Indications center will reach vicinity of Andros Island early Sunday. Hoist northeast storm warnings 10:00 P.M. Fort Pierce to Miami. Increasing northeast winds and probably squalls indicated late Sunday.

Andros Island is just 150 miles east of the Upper Keys, but there was still no hurricane warning. The highest winds reported from the Bahamas that evening were 46 miles per hour.

Just a half hour later, Paul Harris and Oscar Fry, two veterans from Camp 1, bivouacked on Miami Beach—a free room under the stars. Someone nearby who was also taking advantage of the free room owned a tinny radio, which broadcast a report of a small storm near Andros Island heading in a northwesterly direction at eight miles an hour. The two veterans worked up its path. The way they figured it, the storm would head toward the middle of the Florida Keys and right across Upper and Lower Matecumbe. Camp 1 lay right in its course.

CHAPTER FOUR

Sunday
September 1, 1935
to Midafternoon

$\mathcal{E}$arly Sunday morning, at 2:56 A.M., the Jacksonville Weather Bureau issued another advisory:

> Tropical disturbance central about fifty miles west of Long Island, Bahamas, apparently moving westward about eight miles per hour, accompanied by shifting gales and possibly winds hurricane force near center.

Though the Weather Bureau considered 100 miles the minimum diameter of a tropical cyclonic disturbance, this particular storm was more tightly wound than that—perhaps only 40 miles across. A glance at a regional map would have told anyone that the storm was 300 miles east-southeast of the Matecumbe Keys.

Because the hour was early and most telegraph offices were closed, the bulletin didn't receive general distribution. But Colonel Ed Sheeran had already begun his preparations. On his way home to Coral Gables on Saturday night to spend the holiday with his wife, Sheeran had stopped at the drugstore at Tavernier—where the proprietors took phone messages for him—and picked up two callback requests, one from Fred Ghent in Jacksonville and the other from state highway department engineer B. M. Duncan in Key West. Returning both calls, Sheeran found out that the storm was in the Bahamas, much closer than he had heard when he demanded that morning that Sheldon send in the relief train.

Sheeran immediately canceled his holiday plans and drove to the homes of some of his civilian workers in Tavernier, asking them—as well as some tugboat workers he encountered—to report to Camp 3 the next morning at six to help put the construction equipment in hurricane order. W. Z. Burris, a fifty-nine-year-old assistant to Sheeran, arrived at the camp from his Miami home at 3:00 A.M. and started moving the floating equipment into a dredged creek for safekeeping, according to plan.

Down in Key West, meteorologist Gerald Kennedy called Sheldon in his hotel at 5:00 A.M. to report that recent barometric readings were lower in Key West than in Miami, which indicated that the approaching storm's center lay nearer the

Keys than Miami. Since the Straits of Florida are only 95 miles wide, a storm there could be expected to hit Key West with hurricane-strength winds. Further, the Matecumbe Keys, though 75 miles from Key West, are only 20 miles north— hardly enough for comfort. And to make matters worse, the Keys would be in the hurricane's dangerous semicircle—that is, on the right-hand side of its axis of travel, where the system's forward motion would add to the wind speed. Kennedy would say later that he urged Sheldon to return to the camps immediately.

Sheldon got dressed and phoned Ghent in Jacksonville to update him, and Ghent told Sheldon to return to the camps. Sheldon then woke his wife, who got dressed, and they drove the 45 miles to No Name Key to board Captain Albury's ferry. The *Monroe County* departed at 8:00 A.M.

<hr />

Colonel Sheeran spent the night on Lower Matecumbe, sleeping in the state highway department's houseboat anchored in Hurricane Creek, the 1,000-foot dredged channel that now served as a storm anchorage on the Gulf side near Camp 3. Before dawn he got out of his bunk, turned on the radio, and dressed while hearing nothing but talk about the approaching storm. The sun rose, and there wasn't a breath of wind, he later recalled. Sheeran wasn't fooled; he knew that the morning before a hurricane often dawned calm, clear, and beautiful. The barometer was falling slowly.

As he drove up to the Matecumbe Hotel, seven miles away, he saw Conchs boarding up their windows. At Camp 5, Sheeran ran into his secretary, Arthur William Mewshaw, a thirty-seven-year-old out-of-work lawyer from Charlotte, North Carolina. Mewshaw tagged along when the Colonel went into the hotel to talk to Sam Cutler. "We got to get these men out of here," he overheard Sheeran say. Cutler, who was tracking the storm's progress with thumbtacks in a map on the wall, replied that he would put the process in gear.

Like Ed Sheeran, Albert Buck, of Kinston, North Carolina, second in command of Camp 5, found himself drawn to the Matecumbe Hotel, along with Captain E. B. Parker, director of sanitation in the camps. That morning, in the house he shared with a local resident, Buck had checked the barometer before doing anything else. "I know some little bit about the workings of a barometer," he said, and on Sunday "the barometer started dropping; it continued to dropping gradually." At the hotel, he and Captain Parker spoke to Cutler about the danger facing the men. Virtually powerless, since Sheldon officially remained in charge, Cutler couldn't order the relief train himself, but there was one thing he could do. "[He] ordered all three of the canteens to quit selling beer; issued a verbal to myself, and issued written orders to the other two camps, to close the sale of beer in the canteens," Buck recalled. With their supply of alcohol cut off, at least the veterans would be sober enough to herd up and move out together if and when the time came.

The next Weather Bureau advisory, this one a warning, came at 9:30 A.M.:

Tropical disturbance central short distance south of Andros Island moving westward about eight miles per hour attended by shifting gales and probably winds hurricane force small area near center. Indications storm will pass through Florida Straits late tonight or Monday. Caution advised vessels in path. Northeast storm warnings displayed Fort Pierce to Fort Meyer [*sic*].

The Weather Bureau was doing its best with scant data, but the vagueness of the advisories had to be frustrating for anyone trying to nail down the risk to the Keys. The 2:56 A.M. advisory had warned of a possibility of hurricane-force winds near the storm's center. Now that was raised to a probability. What was clear, however, was that the storm was thought to be intensifying.

Meanwhile, the storm had apparently traveled 140 miles over the previous twelve hours while veering from west-northwest to a little south of west. It was 250 miles southeast of the Upper Keys on a track that, if continued, would take it through the Straits of Florida. Storm warnings now extended north from Miami to Fort Pierce, and those warnings also extended to Fort Myers on the Gulf Coast, definitely including the Keys.

At later depositions, men would offer conflicting memories of conditions and events that morning and over the following days, probably from stress, inattention, and the passage of time before depositions were taken.

Camp 1 superintendent Bill Hardaker would later recall that by 9:30 A.M., "It became more obvious that the storm was coming in our direction." Like everyone else in a position of authority in the camps, he went to the Matecumbe Hotel for further instructions. Cutler told him that Sheldon had already found out about the storm the night before in Key West. Hardaker stayed only a few minutes; he had a couple of broken pumps to deal with, and he had to get them fixed.

While making his rounds delivering ice to the camps that morning, Joe E. Edwards ran into someone who'd lived in the tropics for some time. The man looked out to sea, pointed at the waves and said, "That storm is going to hit us." Usually the ocean waves there broke at a rate of a dozen or so per minute and remained low due to the offshore reef. But a hurricane pushes huge, long swells in front of it that break less frequently—perhaps five per minute. When a storm was far away, the man told Edwards, the waves would fan away from its center and hit the distant shore at an angle. But when the storm was close, the waves would break parallel to shore. That morning about five big waves were arriving each minute, and they were breaking parallel to shore. The man's analysis of the swells' orientation was flawed, but he was right about their frequency.

After Colonel Sheeran left headquarters he drove back down to Camp 3 to check on the civilian workers who were putting the dredgers, sand suckers, cement mixers, and other machinery in the hurricane slips dug earlier that year. He told them to get north as soon as they were done. While they moved the pile driver, Sheeran checked the news wires. Wilton Smith, an Islamorada resident who cooked for the twenty-five men on the civilian work crew, walked up behind Sheeran, and before he could say anything, the colonel said, "We are all getting out." Colonel Sheeran was a man who liked to get to the point.

They both listened to the radio, which said the storm was still small but that its course now seemed to be swinging northwest. Both men knew that hurricanes, unless they disintegrate first, eventually head north.

"I am not going out unless the veterans are moved," Sheeran told Smith.

"Colonel, I will stay with you then," Smith replied

"I will certainly appreciate it if you will," Sheeran said.

If the veterans were taken off Lower Matecumbe Key, then they too would follow, he told Smith. Otherwise, they would stay in the channel on the houseboat *Sarasota*— doubtless the most solid structure near Camp 3—and he asked Smith to put a supply of food and water on board just in case. Smith went to the camp commissary and started packing supplies.

At 10:00 A.M. the Weather Bureau repeated but did not update the nine-thirty warning. Meanwhile, as the surf rolled in, speculation about the storm flew around Camp 3. Rumors spread that it had sliced across the northern edge of Cuba. James Lindley, who worked in the kitchen, never heard much more about it than that. In fact, he didn't know anyone in Camp 3 with a barometer, so there was little real information to go on. The nearest barometer he knew of was in an office over by the highway, but no one thought to go over and check it. Veterans all up and down the Matecumbes had grown increasingly curious about the impending storm, however, and some were even excited about the prospect. "We heard Sunday morning that the hurricane warnings were out, up rather," Fred Bommer, Jr., of New York City and Camp 1, said, "and naturally we were all interested in seeing a hurricane or experiencing one, and we all hoped it would blow the mosquitoes away and cool things off."

"All the natives were talking about cyclones, storms, hurricanes, etc.," Jacob S. Herbert of Los Angeles remembered. "Of course, there was a lot of us who didn't know about hurricanes and we were all eyes and ears, but the weather looked just like a threatening ordinary storm. They said not to worry—we would be taken away in time."

A few may have been worried, but no one that Arnold Flow, also from Los Angeles, ran into. And anyway, it didn't bother him. "I figured that the authorities, in case something did happen, they would have transportation there for us," he said. "A train—that was the understanding—there would be a train." His military service, it seemed, had conditioned him not to question authority.

Robert Ayer, Jr., file clerk for FERA at the Matecumbe Hotel headquarters, arrived at the hotel just before lunch. Cutler was still there, still unofficially in charge, and surrounded by ten or so other administrators. "Mr. Cutler is a very nervous sort of fellow," Ayer said. "I mean he imagines things. He was probably the most nervous one there." If he was the most nervous, Cutler had good reason—the two office telephones rang almost constantly. He'd receive a weather report on one telephone or the other, and relay it to Mrs. L. A. Fritchman, who would take it down in shorthand and make copies to distribute. Then he'd stick another thumbtack in the map on the office wall. Even Fritchman thought that Cutler was overreacting. As a Miami resident, she'd been through many a hurricane.

But Sheeran's warning of a bad storm coming—a warning that he repeated around 10:00 A.M.—rang in Cutler's ears. And what worried him most was that he couldn't raise Sheldon on the phone, nor Ghent for that matter. As a last resort he called up the Florida East Coast Railway in Miami and asked them to send down a rescue train. "And they apparently asked him if he had authority to order a train out," Buck said. "He told them that he did not have authority but was going to proceed to get authority, and to hold the train in readiness, and as soon as he got this authority that he would order the train out."

Late that morning in Biscayne Bay, Pilot William Clemmer, a U.S. Coast Guard lieutenant, fired up the engines of a twin-engine General Aviation PJ-2 flying boat and shoved the throttles to the firewall. The airplane moved forward, gathering speed, and as it plowed ahead faster, it lifted on its step and skimmed the waves, then parted from the surface and slowly climbed out. Lieutenant Clemmer banked the airplane slowly and took up a heading south in search of small boats near the shore. Knowing that a tropical storm could easily fill the Straits of Florida, Clemmer's Coast Guard commanders had decided to warn all boats to dock or leave the Keys. Radio-equipped craft were easy to contact, but radio-free craft needed a different system.

The flying boat skimmed above Long Key Fishing Camp, carved out of the sand in 1908 by Henry Flagler, where celebrities such as Zane Grey and President Herbert Hoover had come to fish and "rusticate" over the years. Clemmer descended and circled the shore once, slowly, above a number of small boats. From one of them, Camp 3 veteran Turner Martin, of Gainesville, Florida, looked up in time to see a long streamer tied to a wooden block flutter from the airplane into the ocean. Martin fished out the bobbing block and read on it a message warning of an approaching hurricane. The message asked that the recipient pass it along to other boaters in the area. Overhead, Lieutenant Clemmer dipped the airplane's wings and continued south, dropping more messages to warn other fishermen. When he ran out of blocks, Clemmer banked around and headed back to Miami for more. When the Coast Guard station ran out of blocks, Clemmer dropped ice-cream boxes with streamers fashioned from tape. He didn't drop any boxes or blocks on the camps, however; after all, a telephone line ran through them.

As noon rolled around, Colonel Sheeran went to the only phone in Camp 3, at the ticket seller's office near the ferry landing, and called the Weather Bureau. "One fellow come down [to] ask if he was going to leave," William Kohn, a German, would later recall. "He says, 'Not yet.' He says, 'If we get ready we can call them up to the railroad, a train come down here and get them in six hours.'" A few tourists congregated around the ferry landing, waiting for the *Monroe County* to arrive and take them to Key West. Sheeran told them to go back to Miami, "because he says ferry come down here and going to stay here, because it is plenty of storm," Kohn added.

Just after lunch, Camp 5 superintendent Robinson told a group of his veterans to stay in camp, since the train would arrive early Monday morning, and not to get excited or use the flatbed trucks to get out. He added, though, that they should gather their stuff and be ready to go. Melton Jarrell had on his work clothes, and he asked Robinson if he should change into his good clothes for the train trip.

"Yes," Robinson said. Jarrell walked back to his shack and changed.

Cleveland native Joseph Wojtkiewicz was up at the warehouse in Camp 1, where he saw locals, including a deputy sheriff from Tavernier, loading lifeboats on the platform. They had been working since that morning.

"What are you doing?" he asked.

"Getting ready for it," the deputy said, and added that Wojtkiewicz should get out of there as soon as possible.

Hardaker returned to the Matecumbe Hotel's second floor a little after 1:00 P.M. and found fellow camp director Robinson there, along with file clerk Robert Ayer and Johnny Good and just about every other civilian staff person whom Cutler had been able to call back in from a holiday at home. As they waited out the afternoon, Cutler kept phoning Pan Am and the Weather Bureau for storm reports, and kept trying to reach Ghent in Jacksonville. Hardaker thought he seemed alarmed, yet doing his best to get the rescue train down there.

But sanitation officer Captain Parker wasn't too worried. He did mention that it was squally and he was going to board up his nearby house. None of the civilian staffers seemed too worried either. They only wanted to get back to Miami and take their dates dancing in the evening.

One veteran had been assigned to read the barometer at Headquarters three times a day, but he got too drunk and had stayed over in Miami Saturday night. So Arthur Mewshaw spent the afternoon taking barometric readings and relaying those along with telephone messages from Headquarters to Colonel Sheeran. He'd drive through Camp 3 to get to Sheeran, and each time he did the camp veterans asked about the storm. "I told them it looked bad," Mewshaw said. And the men kept asking Mewshaw when the train would arrive.

Finally, at 2:40 P.M., Cutler raised Ghent on the clubhouse phone at Jacksonville's municipal golf course, where Ghent was playing a round of golf.

"If you will give me authority," he told Ghent, "I will take charge of the situation." Ghent answered that Sheldon was fully instructed as to how to handle the matter, and he was supposed to be back by 1:00 P.M.

"But Sheldon hasn't made it back yet," Cutler replied.

"He will be there, all right," Ghent said, and hung up.

John Good, the thirty-two-year-old general storekeeper for the camps, down from his office in Islamorada, asked Cutler what he would do if Sheldon didn't make it back. Cutler didn't say anything, so Good repeated the question. Again Cutler didn't say a word. He just sat there with his eyes glued to the barometer on Sheldon's desk. It was still in a gradual but steady descent.

At four o'clock the Weather Bureau issued an updated advisory:

Tropical disturbance central about 275 miles east of Havana moving very slowly west or west southwestward probably accompanied by winds of hurricane force over small area near center.

The Bureau hadn't yet received any reports from ships in the storm's vicinity. It could only go on information sent from reporting stations in the Caribbean, Cuba, Florida, and the Gulf. The storm had apparently moved less than 40 miles since the morning advisories, but that was no cause for celebration. A tropical storm that pauses, feeding on the superheated waters beneath it, is a potentially deadly storm.

CHAPTER FIVE

Sunday
September 1, 1935
Late Afternoon and Evening

Even on a good day the ferry could arrive hours late. Some-times it would tie up somewhere between Lower Mate-cumbe and No Name Key for as much as a day at a time, waiting out the weather or a mechanical problem. In windy weather like this, the ferry might not make it back at all. Now, a prop shaft sheered suddenly, the boat slowed instantly, and Captain Albury forged ahead on just one engine. At about four o'clock he finally pulled into the Camp 3 ferry slip, three hours late. Given the weather predictions, he absolutely refused to make the return trip to Key West. From the slip, Albury tele-phoned his boss, who agreed that he should stay right there. Albury had his crew tie up the *Monroe County*, and he turned everyone back. "There must have been a hundred automobiles there to take that ferry," said O. D. Griffin of Camp 3. "[Turned] them all back."

A man asked Albury, "Captain, are you going to go back?"

"No."

"Why?"

"We are tied up with a storm."

"I want to see one of these tropical disturbances."

"I hope you are the only one that sees it."

At 4:30 P.M., Sheldon finally pulled his car up to the hotel. Relieving Cutler at Headquarters, he sat down at his desk, which was covered with the storm warnings that Mrs. Fritchman had taken down. While Cutler apprised him of the situation and of Colonel Sheeran's apprehensions, Mrs. Fritchman sighed with relief at Sheldon's appearance. "I thought [Cutler] was unnecessarily alarmed because the warnings were not alarming. I had been in so many of them I was not excited at all," she said. "[Sheldon] just came in and I admired the businesslike way he took charge of things."

Cutler told Sheldon that he'd ordered the canteens to stop selling beer. Sheldon called the order "silly" and countermanded it. Then he got on the phone to the Weather Bureau for a new update. The hotel office was packed. When Captain Parker came in, he told Sheldon there was definitely going to be a storm, and John Good was particularly emphatic about the dropping barometer. According to Mrs. Fritchman, however, Sheldon didn't ask anyone's advice or opinion, nor did he seek out local residents for their perspectives.

⚬⚬⚬

Many of the Camp 1 veterans received their first storm warning at around four, when proprietor Frederick Snyder locked the camp's canteen on Cutler's orders. This didn't go over well; they hollered at him about not being able to buy beer and cigarettes. Snyder left and walked over to the Snake Creek Hospital, which doubled as Camp 1 headquarters, where Hardaker told him that the storm had veered southwest—though where he might have heard this was unclear—and that it was all right to reopen. Perhaps Hardaker felt that Cutler had no real authority, or perhaps he knew by this time that Sheldon had countermanded Cutler's order. So Snyder retraced his steps and unlocked the store so he could sell beer and cigarettes.

Hardaker had more than closed canteens and complaining veterans on his mind. Two cables on the Atlantic side of the hospital had snapped, and the owner had come down and told him that the building was no longer hurricane-proof. She demanded that the doctors remove all the patients. Hardaker assured her that they would.

During the ball game in Ojus, Eugene Lowkis noticed that O. D. King seemed anxious to get back to the Keys. King operated the Rustic Inn store and gas station less than a half-mile south of the Matecumbe Hotel and was the civilian in charge of the work camp vehicles. After Ojus beat them 5–3, King ordered the players to get on the trucks and hurry straight back to camp.

"What's the rush?" Lowkis asked him.

"I got orders to report back to camp," King said. "Stand by with all the trucks and have the gasoline tanks all filled."

The baseball team set out for the camps, but without catcher Ben Davis, superintendent of Camp 3. He owned a home in Miami and wanted to stay there for the rest of the Labor Day weekend. The trucks drove down to the Matecumbes and into foreboding weather; the closer they got, the darker the clouds loomed.

—⚬⚬⚬—

When Blackie Pugh, top sergeant at Camp 3, first heard of the storm that afternoon, he hopped into a pickup with O. D. Griffin and they drove up to the Matecumbe Hotel. In the second-story offices, Sheldon assured Pugh that there was nothing to worry about, and then phoned Ghent up in Jacksonville.

"From what I could make out of the conversation," Pugh said later, "Mr. Sheldon let it be known that there was no danger on the Keys, but that if any danger did arise he would get in contact with [Ghent] at once." Sheldon then added, "The boys are not very excited down here," though he knew well by then that men like Sheeran, Cutler, and others who had lived through previous hurricanes were indeed alarmed.

Down in Key West, Camp 3 timekeeper Arthur Brown, from Hastings, New York, heard a rumor that FERA and camp administrators were going to ship all the veterans out of the

Matecumbes, so he had a mind to stay put in Key West. But when he went over to Flagler Station to confirm the rumor, no one there could tell him anything for sure, so he decided instead to return to the camp. The train north departed on time, at 5:40 P.M., with around thirty-five other vets on board. As it chugged up the Keys, residents yelled to them through the windows, "How's the weather in Key West?" The veterans arrived in the Matecumbes talking of little besides the approaching storm. They told their campmates that on the ride north they'd seen Conchs boarding up their homes.

William R. Thompson, forty, of Brooklyn, New York, stumbled upon yet another form of weather prediction. Thompson owned a puppy that he'd brought to the camps from Clearwater, Florida. The puppy wouldn't settle down, nor would it play, nor would it stay in Thompson's shack. "Didn't think it was going to be like it was," he said, adding, "I had a feeling about the storm myself."

When Cutler walked out of the front door of the hotel late in the afternoon, he took a steady blast of wind and rain in the face. The safety of the men still on his mind, he looked across the two miles of bridge and road to Camp 5 and thought that Buck should gather the veterans together and prop up the shacks, even though Sheldon had said he was certain the men could be safely aboard a relief train well before anything happened. But Robinson beat him to the punch: he had already organized a few men to prop up the shacks with two-by-fours, and the work continued till evening.

Meanwhile, James Wall saw men boarding up the Matecumbe Hotel, taking down its sign and stashing it in the woods. Wall overheard someone say that the hurricane was 18 miles away and coming through the Keys. It was either a wild rumor or something Wall misheard, but the camps were increasingly on edge. While everyone ate in Camp 5 mess, Robinson came by in his pickup, stuck his head in, and told them that the hurricane had changed course again. Then he ordered them to nail down shutters on each shack.

As the afternoon wore on, Colonel Sheeran and his crew were still putting up their equipment near Camp 3, and Cutler went down to see him.

"[The weather] looks very bad, very bad," Sheeran told him. "This is the worst that I have seen, and I've spent a number of years on the Keys."

"Colonel Sheeran," Cutler said, "if you were in temporary charge down here, would you order that train?"

Sheeran, always laconic, didn't say that he would. He'd already requested that from Sheldon more than twenty-four hours earlier, so what was the point? But he repeated that the weather looked terrible.

When his crew finished anchoring the floating equipment in the canals, Colonel Sheeran told Mewshaw it was time for him to get out—to go to Miami or Homestead or somewhere safe. "I told him I did not feel like going and leaving him and some other men in the office," Mewshaw said. He stayed.

———— ∞ ————

Down in Key West, Ernest Hemingway figured he had until Monday noon at the earliest before the hurricane struck. After writing Sunday morning, he went to the marina that maintained *Pilar* and asked the crew there to haul her out. But they couldn't do it just then—too many other boats were in line ahead of his. So he bought a fortune's worth of heavy hawser ($52) and shifted *Pilar* to what looked to him like the safest place in the Navy Yard—a submarine pen, in fact—tying her up there.

———— ∞ ————

That night it stopped raining, and the clouds took on an ominous copper glow. With the equipment finally "in hurricane order," Sheeran sent his men home. But some, like Mewshaw, elected to stay behind, as did Sheeran himself. He may have had contempt for those jobless, shiftless veterans, but they had fought in the Great War like himself, and to him that meant something. Anyway, he was responsible for the equipment.

Early in the evening, New Yorker George Rough of Camp 1, who worked in the warehouse, ran across John Good, who had spent most of the day in Headquarters. Good told him that the storm was surely going to hit, and they'd all have to evacuate. The only question was when, and he'd let Rough know. After seven-thirty, Good returned and told him the storm would arrive late Monday night or early Tuesday morning.

Bill Hardaker returned to the Matecumbe Hotel that evening, bringing his wife and son along. He and Sheldon were friends outside work, and Sheldon had invited him over after supper to keep an eye on the weather with him. To pass the time, they played cards. At one point Sheldon called Ghent in Jacksonville, and Ghent told Sheldon that two trains were in Miami, already made up and standing by, and they could be there in just three hours. Sheldon then called the Florida East Coast Railway and spoke to district superinten- dent P. I. Gaddis, who said that a train was made up and ready to go and could be there in four hours. Sheldon said the train wasn't needed yet, and that Ghent would order it when the time came. Satisfied, he hung up.

But Ghent and Sheldon both misunderstood what the railroad was telling them. Ghent had assumed since an ex- change of letters in May and June that the railroad would keep an evacuation train in constant readiness, whereas rail- road officials felt they'd committed only to prepare one on request and with twelve hours' notice. Sheldon thought Gad- dis was committing to a four-hour evacuation time regard- less of when the request was made, but Gaddis had been speaking only of the time of Sheldon's call. The northbound train from Key West had just arrived and was in the Miami station with steam up, ready to go. To put together a train at another time was a different proposition, one that would take longer. Gaddis assumed, mistakenly, that Sheldon knew that.

Around nine, Blackie Pugh returned to the hotel and walked in to find Sheldon playing 500 rummy. There was no danger of a hurricane hitting the Keys, Sheldon told him, while Sheldon and his wife and Hardaker and his wife went on playing another game of rummy. Pugh asked Sheldon if he was going to stick around that evening. Yes, Sheldon said, he or someone else would be in the office all night. Thus reassured, Pugh got back in the truck and drove down to Camp 3.

In Walter Bischweitz's shack, Bischweitz and his friends gathered around a midget radio set and listened to the storm warnings. "[It was just] a general warning to people that there was a storm coming and for them not to venture down that way in their cars—toward the Keys," he said.

At the Matecumbe Hotel, Sheldon and Hardaker received the 9:30 P.M. report from Jacksonville:

Tropical disturbance central about 260 miles east of Havana, Cuba, moving slowly westward, attended by shifting gales and probably winds of hurricane force small area near center. Caution advised vessels Florida Straits next thirty-six hours. Northeast storm warnings displayed south of Miami to Fort Meyer [*sic*], Florida.

Since 4:00 P.M., apparently, the storm had advanced just 15 miles. But the foursome kept on playing cards until after 10:00 P.M., when a call came in from Ernest Carson, chief meteorologist at the Weather Bureau's Miami office. Hardaker took the call and later remembered Carson telling him that the storm had changed course from a westerly direction to southwest and would probably pass over Cuba south of Havana and into the Yucatán Channel.

With that, the Sheldons and the Hardakers put the cards away and said good-night. Hardaker and his wife and child went back to their cottage. "In view of the fact that it had turned away from me, I felt a little easier," Hardaker said, "and when I went to bed I told my wife it would miss us altogether and would probably hit up around Tampa or up in that section."

He knew the storm was likely to turn north eventually, but now thought it would pass through the straits first. But no one asked how the Weather Bureau could divine the direction of travel of a storm that, according to reports, had scarcely moved for at least eight hours.

In Sheldon's office, Robert Ayer prepared to bed down in a cot next to the phone. Sheldon came in to say that if the next report from the Weather Bureau, scheduled for 3:30 A.M., was serious, Ayer should wake him up at once. If not, however, it could wait until morning. Then he said good-night and went off to crawl into bed with his wife. Within a few minutes Ayer fell sound asleep.

But while Sheldon and Ayer were sleeping, something happened to the small hurricane, measuring only 40 miles across and with an eye just 8 miles in diameter, that had been virtually stalled some 200 miles southeast of the Matecumbes. Maybe, while sitting still with no upper-atmosphere winds to shred it apart, it inhaled enough energy from the heated waters beneath it—like rocket fuel on a fire—to be utterly transformed. Sometimes that happened, but the process and necessary preconditions were mysterious; even seventy years later, the rapid intensification of a hurricane would remain the biggest blind spot of hurricane forecasting.

Whatever the reason, the storm suddenly exploded in power and intensity, while remaining small in diameter, and started whirling at unfathomable speeds, though there were no reporting stations or ships in the area to record just what those speeds were. While the men in the camps slept, unknown to them or to the Weather Bureau, the storm turned into a monster.

CHAPTER SIX

Monday
September 2, 1935
Morning and Early Afternoon

Robert Ayer was fast asleep when the phone rang in Sheldon's office a little after 3:30 A.M. It was the Weather Bureau. Later, a groggy Ayer couldn't remember the caller's name, but he wrote down the man's report:

> Tropical disturbance 275 miles east of the Havanas moving westward. Beware high tides and strong gales.

The storm that had supposedly veered southwest as of five and a half hours before was now reported east of where it had been the previous evening. Nevertheless, since its track was still predicted to head through the Straits of Florida, the report wasn't alarming enough to wake Sheldon. Ayer went back to sleep.

Albert Buck, top sergeant at Camp 5, rose at 5:30 A.M. and peered outside. "[The] clouds looked so muddy and so close down until it looked like you could reach out and get hold of them," he said. He checked the barometer and stayed with it for about an hour. In that time it fell five points, which was five-hundredths of an inch or roughly 1.5 millibars, a sure indication that the storm was in the neighborhood. He left for a while, and when he came back at eight o'clock, the barometer was still dropping.

Matecumbe Hotel owner Captain Ed Butters recalled early morning conditions very different from those reported by Buck. He remembered a fair sky with a few clouds and a light breeze when he and his son got into his car outside the hotel. He and the boy were going to Miami to see a show. Arriving there at eight-thirty in a steady rain with gusty winds, Butters called his wife, Fern, to see if she was okay. She said she was fine; at the hotel, the sky was still partly cloudy, and there was just a light breeze.

But E. B. Parker, director of sanitation for all three camps, described weather conditions that morning as "squally. We would have showers of rain and it would blow about 35 [miles per hour]; maybe some of it was 40 miles an hour."

These divergent recollections were probably due to the rain bands that announce a hurricane's approach. The bands are spiraling arms of storm clouds accompanied by rain and squalls and separated by gaps of clear, windy weather. The

American Practical Navigator—known as "Bowditch" to generations of mariners, after Nathaniel Bowditch, the author of its first several editions beginning in 1802—describes the approach of a hurricane this way:

> As the fall [of the barometer] becomes more rapid, the wind increases in gustiness, and its speed becomes greater, reaching a value of perhaps 22 to 40 knots. On the horizon appears a dark wall of heavy cumulonimbus, the *bar* of the storm [the outer perimeter of the eye wall]. Portions of this heavy cloud become detached from time to time and drift across the sky, accompanied by rain squalls and wind of increasing speed. Between squalls, the cirrostratus can be seen through breaks in the stratocumulus.
>
> As the bar approaches, the barometer falls more rapidly and wind speed increases. The seas, which have been gradually mounting, become tempestuous. Squall lines, one after the other, sweep past in ever increasing number and intensity.
>
> With the arrival of the bar, the day becomes very dark, squalls become virtually continuous, and the barometer falls precipitously, with a rapid increase in wind speed. The center may still be 100 to 200 miles away in a fully developed tropical cyclone.

In the kitchen at Camp 3, Thomas F. Lannon got thirsty at around 8:00 A.M. and set out for Carson Bradford's store nearby to buy himself a beer. Eight or ten other men were gathered there, and a local fisherman came in. "We are going to have a hurricane here sometime today," he said.

"When is the storm going to land here?" someone asked him.

"I don't know," the fisherman said, "but it will be sometime tonight."

Back at headquarters, Sheldon awoke early and received the three-thirty weather advisory from Ayer. Sheldon figured they still had time—forty-eight hours at least—before the storm arrived in the Keys, if it ever arrived there at all. Chances were good that it might keep on track toward the Gulf of Mexico. Sheldon didn't think there was any danger—not yet anyway.

⁕

Farther north, on the mainland in Homestead, William Johns, a reporter for the *Miami Daily News*, rolled out of bed, got dressed, and drove to his office. Johns's beat started south of Miami and stretched all the way down the Keys, though most of the time nothing went on there: one native knifing another, the occasional automobile accident, notes on celebrities arriving at Long Key's fishing camp. But the previous evening, radio stations WQAM and WIOD had reported the storm heading through the Straits of Florida. Johns had been keeping up with the radio bulletins and calling the Weather Bureau in Miami. "[Of] course I was interested in knowing whether or not the camps were going to be evacuated if the storm came," he recalled. "At no time did I think that the storm would hit before late Monday night or Tuesday." But having lived through all the storms there since 1926—including the September 1926 hurricane that had devastated Miami Beach—Johns also didn't put much credence in the Weather Bureau's predictions. "They never know exactly where those storms are," he explained, "and [this one] was coming up through those straits, and knowing that country down there, I knew they were going to get an awful blow." He vividly remembered the 1929 hurricane that had roared across Key Largo, narrowly missing Homestead.

Though Monday was Labor Day, he drove to his office and phoned Sheldon around 9:30 A.M. to get his reaction. Johns got right to the point.

"How is your weather?" he asked Sheldon.

"It's raining and blowing like hell down here right now," Sheldon said.

"What are you going to do about this evacuation in case the storm hits?"

"I have two trains waiting in Miami that can get down here on about three or four hours' notice," Sheldon said, "and in case it gets too bad, why, we will send for them."

"What's your barometer reading?"

Sheldon said it was 29.87. Johns knew that a falling barometer meant trouble. "The minute that the barometer falls more than, say, five or six points here, especially during September, it is an indication of a storm," he said later. He hung up and phoned the *Daily News.*

Johns had heard the stories about the hurricanes of 1906 and '09 that had passed through the Keys while Flagler was building his Overseas Railway, but even after the Railway was completed, the Keys had remained nearly vacant. A storm in such a thinly populated area was "A Dog Bites Man" story. But with 500 or so veterans camped down there now— doubling the population of the Upper Keys—it was a bigger story: A Man Bites Dog story.

Johns filed a short piece saying that two relief trains were waiting in Miami to rescue the veterans, and it appeared in the noon edition of the *Daily News.* He also told the editor that when the relief trains set out he'd be on the first one. Then he rang up the station agent at Homestead and said he wanted to be on the relief train heading south. The agent said that Johns's call was the first he'd heard about relief trains. Johns asked the agent if he would know when any relief trains left Miami. The agent said yes, he would know. "Well, then, please call me, because I want to get on in there at Homestead," Johns said. "I want to go down there and cover the evacuation of the camps."

At 9:00 A.M. at the 136-foot-tall Alligator Reef Lighthouse five miles off Camp 5—a sea-swept outpost on the barrier reef that fringed the Keys—lighthouse keeper Jones Pervis ran up a second red flag with a black square in the center. The first flag meant a storm warning; the second indicated that a hurricane would likely arrive within twenty-four hours.

The 9:30 A.M. warning from the Weather Bureau stated that the storm was now about 200 miles east of Havana,

> moving slowly westward, attended by shifting gales, probably winds hurricane force, small area near center. Caution advised vessels Florida Straits next twenty-four to thirty-six hours. Northeast storm warning displayed Miami to Fort Myers, Florida.

In the last twelve hours, according to the Weather Bureau, the hurricane had crossed just 60 miles of ocean to a point 150 miles southeast of the Matecumbes.

A half hour later, Camp 3's top sergeant Blackie Pugh arrived at the supply house near Camp 5 for provisions, and he used that as an opportunity to drive across the two-mile road over the waters separating Lower from Upper Matecumbe Key and stop by the Matecumbe Hotel. There, Sheldon showed the anxious Pugh the map he was using to chart the storm's progress. According to the map—the same one Cutler had started on Saturday—the hurricane wouldn't hit for another two days at least at the snail's pace it had been traveling over the previous fourteen hours. "I went back to my company and notified the boys of the same," Pugh said.

More and more men wandered into Headquarters, and unlike Blackie Pugh, they stayed around. Eventually the crowd was standing room only. Unable to get any work done, they began playing poker in Sheldon's office and bridge in the office next door. Once in a while, when Sheldon wasn't talking on the phone, they would deal him in.

O. D. King, the transportation superintendent, had been collecting truck keys since the previous day. He told J. D. McLean of Camp 1 that he was collecting them because the relief train might not show up, and at any minute Sheldon might call him to load up the trucks with vets in an orderly fashion and drive them to Homestead. By 10:00 A.M. King had all the keys—all except those for two trucks slated to carry supplies and rations from Camp 3 and Camp 5 to load on the relief train. "[But] they never did get any rations from Camp 5. This truck driver went down to gas his truck and kept on going to . . . the mainland," Frenchy Fecteau said. At 11:00 A.M., King called Camp 3 timekeeper G. C. Sain at his home in Miami and asked him to find Camp 3 superintendent Ben Davis, who had stayed in his home there Sunday night after the baseball game against Ojus.

"Why?" Sain asked. "Are weather conditions poor?"

"Well, things are not right here," King responded. "Get Davis and get here as quick as possible."

Sain hung up immediately and tracked down Davis. Within thirty minutes they were in Davis's Dodge sedan driving south to Camp 3.

Sheldon's barometer now read 29.81 inches—not low, he said later, though it was a drop of six points since his conversation with William Johns two hours before. He tried calling Ghent in Jacksonville at 11:46, first at the George Washington Hotel and then at the Mayflower Hotel, but Ghent wasn't in either place. He left messages for Ghent to call back. "But there was no need of calling Mr. Ghent for the train," he said. He still didn't believe the storm was imminent.

As for Ghent, he slept in at the Mayflower Hotel until 11:00 A.M. After all, he later testified, it was the Labor Day holiday. He could have added, but didn't, that his boss, Conrad Van Hyning, had told him two weeks before that his job would end in October. A half hour after waking up he went to his office, then out to lunch.

———∞———

At noon a tank car containing 10,000 gallons of fresh water arrived via the last regular train to leave the mainland. The train crew parked it at one of the Camp 3 sidings, and veteran Benjamin Meyers found Colonel Sheeran to tell him the car had arrived. Sheeran paused, then told Meyers that it would be better to keep the water on the car instead of pumping it into ground-level storage tanks where it could become contaminated if the sea rose. That way, in case of storm surge, they could at least be assured of fresh drinking water.

At Headquarters, sheets of rain plunged from a low, black sky, squalls blew, and things grew more tense with each

passing minute. A couple of FERA administrators—Paul Vander Schouw, assistant director of Florida's transient division,
and Leila Baggs, supervisor for the transient division's case-
workers—arrived by automobile from Miami to inspect the
camps, despite the wind and rain and the Labor Day holiday. They were just sitting down to have lunch in the Matecumbe Hotel dining room when Cutler bumped into them.
Vander Schouw knew Cutler from when Cutler had been the
camps' safety inspector, and he had a lot of respect for him.
While they talked, Sheldon walked downstairs and joined
them. After a while someone came down from upstairs,
leaned over, and told Sheldon he was wanted on the telephone. Excusing himself, Sheldon trotted up the steps to take
the call in his corner office. When he left, Cutler said to Vander Schouw and Boggs, "This thing looks bad to me and I
want to go on record with you. If I don't see you again or if
anything happens, [I wanted] to get these men out of here."

In his office, Sheldon found Ghent on the line. It was
1:37 P.M. Since Sheldon's phone call two hours earlier, the
hotel barometer had dropped another six points, from 29.81
to 29.75. Sheldon told Ghent as much, and of the squalls of
rain and gusts of wind. Ghent had already received the noon
barometer readings at Key West and Miami from the Weather
Bureau at Jacksonville. They were the only readings Jacksonville had; the personnel from reporting stations at Nassau,
Havana, Fort Pierce, and Tampa had Labor Day off. "While I
was talking with Mr. Ghent," Sheldon said, "the broadcast of
the Weather Bureau came in." The radio broadcast said:

Hoist hurricane warning 1:30 P.M. Key West district. Tropical disturbance central noon about latitude 23 degrees 20 minutes, longitude 80 degrees 15 minutes, moving slowly westward. It will be attended by winds hurricane force in Florida Straits and winds of gale force Florida Keys south of Key Largo this afternoon and tonight.

The eye, according to this report, was 118 miles south and a little east of the Matecumbes, just off the coast of Cuba.

Sheldon asked Ghent to order the relief train, and Ghent hung up. Moments afterward, at 1:45, Sheldon called the dispatcher and told him that Ghent was going to call to order the train. "He had me hold the wire until that call was verified," Sheldon said. He remained on the line for twenty minutes before the dispatcher received the word from Ghent. The dispatcher came back on Sheldon's line and told him the train would be there between five and five-thirty. All Sheldon had to do now was have Hardaker, Davis, and Robinson collect the men in their camps and get them packed and fed by around 4:00 P.M., then have them wait together in the mess tents for the train.

Months earlier, in an exchange of letters, Ghent and the Florida East Coast Railway had agreed that the railroad would send at least one relief train in the event of a hurricane—Ghent apparently thought the railroad had agreed to send two—and only the day before Sheldon had understood a railroad dispatcher to be assuring him a train was ready. On Sunday Ghent had spoken with the dispatcher and told him that the camps "would probably want a train on short notice" with ten coaches and three baggage cars. But now the dispatcher could only come up with a single train made up of six coaches and three baggage cars (weighing somewhere between 75 and 100 tons each), the tender, and the engine—the 160-ton-plus "Old 447." The veterans would be crammed like canned sardines inside the six coaches, but there would be enough room, if only barely. After he ordered the train, Ghent packed his bag at the Mayflower Hotel and prepared to meet the train in Hollywood, where he'd help get the men settled in evacuation quarters. He stopped to fill up at a gas station before leaving Jacksonville, and decided to have the oil changed as well. It was a long drive down to Hollywood—340 miles.

Tired of waiting, some of the men in the work camps had already grabbed their suitcases and grips and started walking north along the train tracks. On the opposite side of Snake Creek, the narrow cut between the Atlantic and Florida Bay separating Windley Key from Plantation Key to its north, veteran Guy Prentiss was walking south, down toward Camp 1. He met a salesman driving north in a new Dodge Coach.

"Do you belong to this camp?" the salesman asked.

"Yes."

"You had better get out," the salesman said. "I heard an

hour ago another storm would hit here at six-thirty and would get worse all night."

In the camps, the wind increased to around 40 miles per hour, a strong gale. The waves that the hurricane pushed in front of it started breaking over the Atlantic shore with more intensity at noon, and at one-thirty the water was at least six inches above Tarvia Road between Camp 5 and Camp 1. Whale Harbor, separating Upper Matecumbe from Windley Key between the two camps, was also inundated.

John Good was near the Matecumbe Hotel sometime after one-thirty when he saw Colonel Sheeran talking to Ray Sheldon. Though only 10 feet away, Good couldn't hear their conversation, but immediately afterward he asked Colonel Sheeran about it. "Evidently Captain [sic] Sheeran advised that we were going to have the kind of a storm those camps wouldn't stand and his advice convinced Mr. Sheldon," Good explained. The shacks—all of the camp buildings, in fact—were constructed from flimsy timber. Some weren't even anchored to the ground. Hurricane-force winds would blow them away like tiny houses spilling off an upset Monopoly board. And finally the colonel was sure that Sheldon understood that.

At 1:00 P.M., O. D. King ran into Frenchy Fecteau, whom he knew from working at Headquarters. King advised him to get out of Matecumbe in his pickup. Having collected the keys to most of the camp vehicles, King returned to Headquarters and gave them to Sheldon. Then he drove to R. O. Grubbs's shack between the Matecumbe Hotel and Islamorada and told him to get his "family ready and he would pick me up and carry me up to his place," Grubbs said. But then King reconsidered—maybe he didn't think his hurricane-proof house could hold all his own relatives along with Grubbs's family—and told Grubbs it would be better instead for him to wait for the train at the Snake Creek Hospital. So King drove them all up there before heading home to Islamorada.

———

Today we have radar, hurricane hunter airplanes, and real-time satellite imagery with which to track a storm from birth to death, monitor its wind speeds, chart its course by the second. We can drop probes in an eye wall to measure pressures and wind speeds. Yet despite these tools and a plethora of computer models with which to predict a hurricane's future track, modern forecasts err by an average of 150 miles over forty-eight hours and 200 miles over seventy-two hours. In 1935 a barometer was about the only tool for predicting hurricanes. With readings from several different stations, the Weather Bureau could extrapolate a hurricane's position. Taken over time, they could estimate its speed. But it was a black art, and never more so than when a hurricane spun up in a remote area.

Yet Sheldon extrapolated the march of thumbtacks across the map on his wall forward into the storm's predicted track as if its future course were as well known as its past, and planned accordingly. He was hardly the first to make that mistake, nor would he be the last.

Based on barometric extrapolations at 12:30 P.M., the men at the Weather Bureau in Jacksonville, Walter J. Bennett and Gordon E. Dunn, thought the storm might have changed direction from west to northwest. But by one-thirty, with additional reports in hand—though none from Havana, where the observer had the day off—they once again thought it was heading slowly westward.

After lunch, Richard Lawrence Bow, a construction engineer on the bridge below Camp 3, returned to the state highway department's houseboat anchored in Hurricane Creek. Comparing the barometric readings the Weather Bureau was reporting from Key West, Miami, and Camp 3, he saw that the lowest reading was in Camp 3, and he estimated that the storm's center might be 80 to 90 miles due east. He sent Bill Smith to tell Sheeran that "if the camp crew didn't have their train on the way, it was time they were getting out." Of all the conflicting reports of the hurricane's position that day, Bow's estimate was most nearly on target.

When a hurricane forms in the tropical North Atlantic or Caribbean, it has a tendency to follow the warm waters of the North Equatorial and Antilles currents. The former flows northwestward through the Caribbean Sea, then north through the Yucatán Channel into the Gulf of Mexico. The latter, an offshoot, flows northwest along the north coast of Cuba and through the Bahamas. The two recombine where the North Equatorial Current, now called the Florida Current, rushes east through the Straits of Florida at four knots or more, and the result is the Gulf Stream, which has been likened to a mighty river in the sea. The Stream flows northward up the East Coast of the United States to Cape Hatteras, where it swerves northeastward to head off across the North Atlantic toward Europe. When a storm traveling westward over the Antilles Current meets the Gulf Stream north of Cuba, its momentum might carry it into the Gulf of Mexico. But if the storm is moving slowly enough, it might instead swing north with the Gulf Stream, toward the Keys.

Around noon this hurricane, which had hovered off the Cuban coast while growing from a garden-variety storm into an intense, tightly coiled killer, took a sharp right turn and headed northwest, toward the Matecumbes. But the Weather Bureau didn't know that yet.

CHAPTER SEVEN

Monday
September 2, 1935
Afternoon

Until 1:30 P.M., Frederick Snyder's day had been like any other except for the weather. He opened the Camp 1 canteen early as usual, then closed down at 9:00 A.M. when the veterans would normally leave for work. He reopened at 11:00 A.M.—when the veterans typically came back for lunch—and worked till 1:30 P.M.—when the veterans' lunch break was usually over. But then things turned strange, and not just because it was Labor Day or because the weather was increasingly hostile. On his way out the door, Snyder ran into Captain Hardaker, who wore a yellow raincoat and sea hat. Hardaker's wife and children were getting ready to leave in Hardaker's car. Snyder saw that one of the tires was nearly flat, and he told Hardaker's wife that she'd need air in it if she was going far.

"By the way," Hardaker said to Snyder, "go into the canteen and get all the money counted. . . . Hooks [who was in charge of all the canteens] will be along from the office and get it." Then he told Snyder to get his clothes packed—they were going to evacuate soon.

Snyder went back into the canteen and was just unlocking it when Hooks drove up in a big hurry. The two men got the money out, along with the laundry money and laundry slips. "[Hooks] marked it all up, but we forgot all about my money that was in the safety deposit drawer of the cash register," Snyder said. They also nailed down the windows, and Hooks took Snyder's register keys.

"[If] the wind [starts] up, [we'll] send in a truck and take [the register] to Islamorada so it [will] not be destroyed," Hooks said.

Snyder went to his barracks and retrieved his belongings, then returned to the supply house. There, the strengthening wind tore loose an upper corner of the house, so he grabbed a ladder, climbed up, and nailed it down. From that vantage point, with the wind hitting his face, it looked like the sea had begun to rise. He climbed down and buttonholed another fellow to help him pick up supplies off the floor and put them on benches to keep them dry. Then they heard that the cooks were handing out sandwiches and coffee at the mess tent, so they hurried over there.

In the mess, at around 1:00 P.M., the staff had just cleaned up from lunch and started cooking supper when Captain Hardaker came in and told them to stop fixing the soup or anything else they had on the stove. "Open canned goods and feed the men immediately," he told them. Hardaker also ordered them to pack enough rations for three full meals and enough dishes and china to serve all of Camp 1. The provisions would be needed in their temporary evacuation headquarters.

Around one-thirty, as vet Roy Hurley walked the few hundred feet from Camp 1 to Snake Creek Hospital, he saw Frederick Snyder closing the canteen. In the hospital, he saw the three doctors huddled in conference. Dr. Alexander volunteered to ride with the men on the relief train so that Dr. Main could drive Hardaker's wife and son into Miami, but Dr. Main wouldn't hear of it; he, after all, was the senior doctor in camp. He said that Dr. Ayers should drive out instead. "I'm going to stay here and see the excitement," Dr. Main told them. Dr. Alexander said he'd also stay in camp through the storm. Four vets who worked in the hospital decided they'd stay too. Pinochle players all, they joked about playing by candlelight if the electricity went out.

At about two o'clock Dr. Ayers got into the car with Captain Hardaker's family and started north. At three-fifteen the ambulance loaded with the hospital's four patients—including Frank Latach of Camp 3, one of the few skilled veterans working on the bridge down there, who'd injured his chest the day before—pulled out and headed north as well, with James L. King at the wheel. At three-thirty a Mr. Cash, who worked in the hospital, said to Dr. Main, half in jest, "If the company's cars and trucks have to be taken out of here, suppose I drive your car up to Miami?"

"Do that," Dr. Main replied unexpectedly, adding, "deliver it to me when the train arrives." Walter Smith and a vet named Legaras also wanted to go, and Roy Hurley told Dr. Main he'd like to go too.

"Yes, you go on," Dr. Main said, "and keep sober."

Hurley had two suitcases, one too many to fit in the car, so he left one inside the hospital, along with his tennis racket. When he crawled into the car, Dr. Main told them to roll the windows down. They did, but they didn't know why. Still, they thought it best not to question a doctor.

As they started off it rained even harder, and the wind blew "just about strong enough to begin to know that you had something in the air, just much more than just a plain wind," Hurley said. When they crossed the Snake Creek Bridge, Hurley realized why Dr. Main had told them to keep the windows down: the car might otherwise have slid right off the bridge's slippery planks.

Just after King told him to leave the Keys, Frenchy Fecteau drove to his little seven-shack community on Upper Matecumbe Key and loaded up the whole Van Ness family, his neighbors there. Diving north while the rain buffeted his truck, he was stopped below Snake Creek by Monroe County deputies firing their guns across the road. Fecteau didn't need more incentive than that. He stopped and rolled down his window for the slickered sheriff, who leaned in through the driving rain to get closer.

"What's the idea?" Fecteau yelled.

"Well, I will tell you, Frenchy," the sheriff yelled back. "I have got orders from camp headquarters to stop all veterans; there will be a train here at four o'clock in the afternoon."

Fecteau rolled up the window and turned to the Van Nesses. "Will I rush for him or stop?" he asked them.

"We might as well stop," Ben Van Ness said. "If the train will be here in two hours, we can go the rest of the way in the train, because we can go faster in the train than the car."

Against his better judgment, Fecteau turned around and drove over to nearby Snake Creek Hospital. Everyone emptied from the truck and ran inside.

At two-thirty Ed Butters called his wife, Fern, from Miami, to ask how things were in the Upper Keys. "Well, if you want to know the truth," she said, "it's blowing like hell here."

"I'm on my way," Butters answered.

*

In Homestead around midday the weather grew more insistent, the rain slamming in from the east on winds of 30 to 40 miles per hour. Reporter William Johns of the *Miami Daily News* continued to check in with the Weather Bureau, which kept stating through the early afternoon that the hurricane was 200 miles east of Havana and headed west through the Straits of Florida.

On the Matecumbe Keys the wind increased between 1:00 and 2:00 P.M. On Long Key, J. E. Duane, caretaker for the fishing camp there and one of the Weather Bureau's cooperative observers, recorded a falling barometer, a high tide, and a heavy swell at 2:00 P.M. The wind was from the north or northeast, but only 25 to 31 miles per hour there at the time, in a lull between squalls. That would soon change.

Camp 3 timekeeper G. C. Sain and camp leader Ben Davis finally reached O. D. King's home in Islamorada from Miami just before 2:00 P.M. "There, Mr. Davis received a written communication from the Matecumbe office stating that a train was on the way and to reach camp as quickly as possible to prepare our men with bedrolls and provisions to entrain," Sain recalled. Within a half hour Sain and Davis arrived at the Camp 3 mess hall, where Davis fought the blowing wind to get inside. Soaking wet, covered with sand, he told the mess sergeant and his crew to brew coffee and make sandwiches for the men to eat at 4:00 P.M., and then pack up the utensils, plates, silverware, and canned goods and get ready to load them on the train. He called Peter J. Larkin, who ran the camp infirmary, and told him to pack all of his drugs and bandages in the ambulance and get it ready to roll. Larken crammed it full. Then Davis drove his Dodge back up the length of Lower Matecumbe Key and across the bridge to see Ray Sheldon in the Matecumbe Hotel. Sheldon told him to expect the train to arrive by five-thirty but assured him they had plenty of time. The Weather Bureau's one-thirty prediction was that the worst of the weather would not arrive for another ten or so hours. Sheldon still believed he was taking precautions against a storm surge and storm-force winds—not against a direct hit from a hurricane.

Davis told Sheldon that he planned to put Blackie Pugh in charge of the Camp 3 men on the train, and he would drive his new car out alongside it. Sheldon told him no, he should go with the veterans and let office worker George Pepper drive his car out with some of the women. Davis went out to his car and unloaded his Army trunk to give the passengers more room, then handed the keys over to Pepper and wished him luck. It would be the last time he saw his brand-new Dodge sedan.

Davis got into a truck with Sain and they drove at high speed back down to Camp 3 and the mess tent. He ordered the few men gathered there to fan out to the shacks and tell the veterans to head to the mess tent. He needed everyone together when the train pulled in. Next, Davis went to the power plant, where veteran L. W. McNamara was running things. Davis told him, "Try to keep the power going as long as you can." He assured McNamara that the train would arrive at five-thirty, just as Sheldon had told him, and then he left. Right afterward, Colonel Sheeran came in and told McNamara to shut off the water pump—they wouldn't need fresh water for a couple of days. And Sheeran added, "I think you men will go on the trucks." McNamara felt reassured; either way, train or trucks, they were getting out.

At about three-thirty Davis had Blackie Pugh set off the mess hall siren—it normally blew only for food service—and the men struggled through the rain and wind and sand to get to the tent. "Roll up your mattresses and get ready to leave," Captain Davis said. The train was not due for two hours.

After Pugh sounded the siren, W. H. Turner came up to him to say he wished he'd made it into Miami that Saturday to see his sister.

Turner wouldn't live through the night.

———— ✇ ————

At 3:00 P.M., J. E. Duane on Long Key noted that the wind was still in the north to northeast and rising, but large waves were rolling in from the southeast—a strong indication that the storm had moved north. On Upper Matecumbe, Sheldon still assumed the hurricane would pass to the south, but he began thinking that the relief train's scheduled 5:30 P.M. arrival was cutting things uncomfortably close to the coming storm surge and high winds. He resigned himself to waiting it out, but was determined to get the Headquarters staff and their families to safety. Sheldon took aside Robert Ayer, the FERA file clerk who had manned the phone in Sheldon's office the night before, and told him to pack a suitcase. He advised Ayer to drive north to Hollywood with Mrs. Ayer and wait there for the relief train to arrive on its return journey north. Then he handed Ayer the keys to his own car.

"To tell you the truth," said Ayer, "some people down there had never seen a storm and wanted to stay there and see what happened." Not Ayer. He and his wife left the hotel.

At three-thirty, with the weather growing steadily worse, Sheldon told Sam Cutler to drive up to Hollywood and find a place to put the veterans when they arrived on the relief train. They would need water, enough space for tents, and sanitary facilities. Then Sheldon loaded his wife, Gayle, in a caravan of five cars full of office workers and sent them north through the roadblock he had asked the sheriff to set up below the Snake Creek Bridge to prevent the veterans from leaving. Sheldon wanted to keep the veterans together in order to load them on the train in an orderly fashion when it arrived. The five cars pulled out on the road in the pouring rain with their lights on and set off north. The deputy let them through—the cars were carrying civilians, after all.

At 4:00 P.M., Sheldon phoned up the railroad in Miami and asked about the train. It was on its way, the dispatcher assured him. At the same time, on Long Key, J. E. Duane recorded winds of 47 to 54 miles per hour from the north, continuing rain, and the barometer was dropping a heart-stopping hundredth of an inch every five minutes.

In Camp 1, veteran William Hellman stared out toward the Atlantic, thinking about all the storms he'd seen in his Navy days. As he watched, the seas reared up and thundered toward the shore, spreading white foam in all directions as the waves broke on the beach. "This storm is about hitting us now," Hellman said to a man standing beside him. "Why don't we go up and steal one of these damn trucks and wheel a bunch of men and take them with us, because that thing is coming?"

"No," the man said, adding, "I'm scared." He didn't say whether he was afraid of the storm or of the ramifications of stealing a truck. In a few hours he would be dead.

Throughout the camps, other veterans considered stealing trucks to escape. Mechanic John Dombrauski of West Virginia and his friend Adam Rambowski from Virginia went to the Camp 3 garage with some other drivers to take the keys. When they arrived they found Colonel Sheeran's bookkeeper, Sergeant Nushow, guarding the garage. But there was nothing the colonel or Nushow could do about their own pickup. Dombrauski and Rambowski hot-wired it and drove off around 4:00 P.M. in road conditions that would have suited the Western Front. By the time they got to Snake Creek Bridge, its sides were already washed out. "We heard a kind of wiggling as we drove over," Dombrauski said. How they got past the roadblock wasn't clear. They made it into Homestead.

A few others made it out in private vehicles. Sixty-two-year-old Frederick Poock, of Homestead, office manager and trust officer at Headquarters, offered to stay with Sheldon, but Sheldon told him to leave; the more who got out in vehicles, the more room there would be for veterans on the crowded relief train. Poock saw men playing penny ante poker in the office. "Everyone I think was more or less on edge," he said, "and I think they were playing cards to break the waiting spell between [telephone] calls. It was really a pastime and not a real poker game." Men would walk up and join and leave again. Eventually Poock decided to take Sheldon's advice, and he left with Captain Wigginton in Wigginton's car, leaving behind the veterans' financial records.

O. D. King had told garage foreman Jay MacDonald to drive as many of the women and children out as he could. McDonald and the women he managed to corral left Camp 5 at 4:00 P.M., reaching Homestead and safety. To get the rest of the women and children closer to the train, King asked Lloyd Everett to drive them up to the hospital. "I suggested to Mr. King that we use my stake body truck to bring the women from [Matecumbe]," Everett said. "He stated that he had the keys to all the trucks and had orders not to release them." Everett ended up making three round-trips in his small ton-and-a-half truck.

By four o'clock Albert Buck, general foreman of Camp 5, had a growing feeling that the train wasn't going to come in time. Robinson, the camp superintendent, told him to take his pickup and head out with his family. Buck asked Robinson to come with him. "No," Robinson said, "I am going to stay with the men and I will make that train when it goes out, if it gets here." Because he was a camp sergeant, Buck got through the roadblock. At about the same time, Blackie Pugh, the Camp 3 top sergeant, told Sheldon that if the men weren't given transportation out soon they'd leave on their own. If they did, Sheldon replied, they'd be stopped and turned back.

In Camp 1, the cooks prepared a last meal. "We opened up canned beans and corned beef and fed the boys," said Grover C. Raines.

"Then we ran back into our quarters to get anything we wanted to take with us," Albert Pawa of Newark, New Jersey, said. "I put a few things into my grip and got ready to go." One by one the vets arrived in the mess hall and ate lunch. The men nailed their doors and windows shut, as Captain Hardaker had asked them to do. When he blew the siren again at three-thirty, around 150 men gathered inside the mess tent. At four o'clock Hardaker asked for a volunteer to drive his truck to Hollywood, where the train was going to stop on its way north. Snyder volunteered, but Hardaker refused. "No, I want you here," he told him. "You are big and husky and I need you." But Hardaker soon reconsidered and told Snyder to walk over to the hospital and wait for a deputy sheriff to arrive with his truck.

Snyder pulled away from the hospital with another man, whom he referred to as "the little fellow," late in the afternoon, heading for Hollywood. Snyder later remembered leaving at 5:30, but it was probably closer to 4:30. Since they were in Hardaker's personal vehicle, the deputies let them through.

According to eyewitness reports from a few veterans, the relief train had been made up for hours—since early that morning, some said. The railroad just needed permission from Ghent to send it out, which he had given just before 2:00 P.M. "I felt we could move this train into the area within three hours, load the men within an hour and move them back to the mainland within another hour and a half," Ghent said later.

It didn't quite work that way. After getting Ghent's go-ahead, the railroad dispatcher had to call in a crew. On a holiday, that took time—over an hour. Engineer J. J. Haycraft got the call to report for duty at 3:10 P.M. at his home in Miami. An oil-burning engine like Old 447 needed about an hour to get up steam. It finally departed the Miami station for Homestead at 4:25, then had to halt for at least ten minutes when a drawbridge tender opened the bridge spanning the Miami River to allow sailboats and yachts into their berths.

At three-fifty reporter Johns got the call he'd been awaiting from the Miami station agent, saying that the train would soon pull out and would reach the Homestead station in about an hour. He battled the wind and the stinging rain out to his car, then fought them both again driving to the station.

In its four-thirty bulletin, the Weather Bureau finally caught up with the storm's new track:

Tropical storm now apparently moving northwestward towards Florida Keys accompanied by hurricane winds over small area. Hurricane warnings displayed Key West and town of Everglades, and northeast storm warning elsewhere south Florida coast West Palm Beach to Sarasota.

That information was two hours old.

By 5:00 P.M. the train finally rolled into Homestead, but no sooner had it arrived than Engineer J. J. Haycraft decided to back the train down the Keys. He and the crew turned the engine around and switched it from front to back, coupling it by the nose to the cars. Haycraft's plan was to move the engine to the front of the train on a siding once they reached the camps and chug out in the normal fashion, with the locomotive's headlight showing the way through the darkness on the return trip. The switch ate up another thirty minutes, during which time eight veterans, including Hollis Morris from Camp 5, arrived from the Keys in an old Ford Model A that was just running out of gas. They told Johns and Haycraft that they'd left their clothes back at camp and now figured it would be quicker to take the train back into the camps from Homestead and then ride it to Miami than to drive the same route. They did not explain how all eight of them had managed to forget their clothes.

While the train was in Homestead, J. E. Duane on Long Key recorded winds of hurricane strength. At five-thirty, as the train backed out, the wind was blowing hard and the water started breaking over bridges and submerging roads. On board, Conductor J. E. Gamble told a couple of veterans that the train could already have been to Islamorada and back. The problem, he said, was that the railroad wanted the government to pay $300 for the relief train, and Ghent didn't want to pay it. If the dispatcher and Ghent hadn't spent hours arguing, he explained to the men, they would have been picked up. Hearing this, which was probably an unfounded rumor, the veterans grew incensed and repeated the story to the others riding down to the camps.

Before the relief train reached Key Largo, the sky turned black. When the train backed over the narrow strip of land known as Cross Key, which connected Key Largo with the mainland, waves were leaping two to three feet over the tracks. On Key Largo the sky lightened somewhat, but before Tavernier, the wind blew with greater ferocity and the rain pelted harder. On Plantation Key the train once again plunged into darkness.

❊

At the Matecumbe Hotel, Sheldon took supper with other FERA staff and Monroe County chief deputy sheriff Louis Maloney. Maloney and other deputies would help load the veterans onto the train, and Sheldon wanted them to do it as quickly as possible. While they were talking, Ed Butters and his son arrived, having completed a white-knuckle 80-mile drive from Miami in a rising tailwind. Then Maloney and Sheldon got into the deputy's car with Olin Perdue, night watchman at the grocery warehouse, and D. A. Malcolm, chief project auditor, and drove in second gear to the Isla-

morada train station to board the southbound train and supervise the boarding of the veterans. Mahoney estimated that
the wind was blowing between 60 and 70 miles per hour
when they arrived between five and five-thirty.

While the wind howled, Camp 1 veteran Patrick
Howard, from New York City, left his shack and ran into
Leo Moran, and they both leaned forward and stumbled
through the blinding rain toward the Snake Creek Bridge.
There they met the sheriff's deputies, who told them that
Dr. Main said it was unsafe outside and that the doctor had
ordered everyone to report to the hospital. Retreating to the
hospital, they found it full of children, women, and men—
all of them anxiously waiting for the relief train. Ben Van
Ness, his wife, Laura, and their four kids cowered in one
room, along with a veteran from Camp 5 with his wife and
child, two Camp 1 veterans, and a new employee of the infirmary. Six men crouched in a second room. Howard and
Moran joined the crowd.

As the afternoon wore on and the storm worsened, others
took their own initiatives to get away.

Forty-year-old veteran William R. Thompson from Brooklyn decided to abandon Camp 5. It was too low and narrow
to last through a hurricane; water was already up to the canteen. Thompson figured the best direction to head was toward Camp 3. He tried to recruit some of the other vets to
go with him, but there was only one taker—a fellow named
Cunningham. Thinking they could catch the relief train when
it went by, they walked out along the railroad.

William S. Belk and John Storey, of Camp 5, and a fellow they knew only by his last name, Byers, caught a ride on a laundry truck heading out of the Keys and nearly made it to Homestead. "I got knocked off on this long bridge at Homestead," Storey said. "That is where the laundry truck blowed off it."

In Camp 1, some of the veterans waited in the mess tent for more than two hours, according to James C. Morrison, while others returned to their shacks. Morrison remembered Hardaker telling them, "This thing is going to blow over. I think you fellows had better get to your cabins and stay there."

Loray O'Donnell recalled it differently: "The dining room began to shake and [Hardaker] ordered us all to our barracks." O'Donnell said that Hardaker didn't seem to think the mess hall could stand much longer.

By the time Captain Hardaker made the rounds of the shacks at 5:10 P.M. to give a twenty-minute warning for the train's hoped-for arrival, objects—washtubs, even—were flying around outside. A few men ran to the mess tent, where one picked up a can of soup to eat later: "When we seen how terrible it was getting . . . I thought I could miss a meal or two," said Jacob S. Herbert. "I come originally from Pennsylvania, and I got to thinking about the Johnstown flood." That disaster had occurred in May 1889, when a dam in a reservoir 450 feet above Johnstown burst and 20 million gallons of water poured down on the unsuspecting city of 30,000. More than 2,200 people died, while thousands more ended up without shelter, clean water, or food for days. With that can of soup, Herbert steeled himself for the worst.

In Hurricane Creek, aboard the houseboat *Sarasota*, Colonel Sheeran noted winds of 60 miles per hour at five o'clock, increasing to 125 miles per hour before six, then building further. An increase from 60 to 125 miles per hour in thirty minutes was something, he said, "which I never saw before in my life." He had about thirty people with him on the *Sarasota*.

One Camp 3 veteran, Floridian John Skularicos, took his picture of Jesus down from his shack. "I tell the boys," he said, "I like to get down and pray for the God to save your life; for the storm come now, I wish you fellows get better places, this is going out in fifteen minutes if the storm come; the wind got the other way; and everybody listen to me; nine kiss the Christ and live, and two don't and die. This is true." He and "the boys," though, got out of his shack and ran to a nearby Studebaker, which was parked facing into the wind, and hunkered down inside.

About five o'clock, Captain Robinson finished making the rounds of each shack in Camp 5, telling everyone to nail down whatever they could and then to gather at the mess hall to evacuate. As the men started leaving the shacks with their bags, the wind suddenly burst in with renewed power and lifted their shacks off the ground. The one next to James A. Wall's shack collapsed, and then his shack jumped a foot and a half off its foundation. "We thought it was time to get out," he said.

Then the mess hall collapsed with Robinson inside. A timber fell on him, and Robinson became the first man known to have died in the camps.

In contrast to the shacks, which were tumbling away, the food supply building by Camp 5 stood firm. Designed to be stormproof, it had been built with pillars buried three feet deep and set in concrete, had double floors and was triple braced on top.

George Hill was climbing to the top when the first wave caught him. It carried him 120 feet before his clothing got caught on a pole. Looking back, Hill watched the supposedly stormproof building wash away with men still inside. In a few seconds it disintegrated. The pole to which he was attached floated southwest more than a mile and a half before he got snagged by yet another pole. A woman washed by him, and he tried to grab her by her dress, but the current was too strong for his grip. She was swept away.

As five o'clock approached at Camp 3, the veterans gathered their gear from the shacks and fought the rain and sand and high wind to the mess hall. There, they waited. Some ate the weenie sandwiches and cheese sandwiches the cooks made; they'd already packed up the rest of the food. All the men crammed inside, someone passed around a bottle, and the huddled gathering turned into a party of sorts, with drinking, joking, and singing over the storm's roar. Most of the men came from the North and West and so had never been through a hurricane before. And anyway, they'd heard it wasn't due for a long, long time. "And we was all kidding about the storm was going to land, and the train would be there sure by five," said Thomas Lannon.

But five-thirty came and went, and still no train. The wind blew stronger and harder—camp leader Ben Davis estimated it was blowing at nearly 150 miles per hour—and the tent rattled with sand pounding the canvas. The men's joking grew nervous, and then it stopped. It seemed that something had gone seriously wrong. Twenty or thirty veterans were now gathered in the mess hall, and things began to look desperate. Davis ordered them to forget loading their gear on the train when it came: just jump on board and forget anything else.

Camp 3 timekeeper G. C. Sain was a Keys local, and he knew a thing or two about hurricanes. "I busied myself as much as possible instructing the boys how to conduct themselves in case the train did not get in to us," he said, "informing all who were not familiar with tropical hurricanes that they worked in circles, and we would get a backlash or second storm, which would be equally hard, if not harder, than the first, and all would have to stay in—never venture out." Despite this advice the men started to panic.

At 6:00 P.M. on Long Key, J. E. Duane recorded a barometric pressure of 28.04, still falling. The rain was heavy, the wind still building. In Camp 3, the hurricane screamed so loudly it seemed to be right outside. The low air pressure outside assaulted the higher pressure trapped inside the tent, and without warning the tent seemed to explode.

"Every man for himself!" Davis, in his later deposition,

remembered screaming, but no one could hear him above the storm. The lightbulbs exploded while stinging rain whipped the vets. "Then," Sain said, "we were scattered like a flock of quail."

The wind picked up several of the men and flung them into the darkness like waste paper. The rest were hit by splintered wood and timber and anything else that wasn't tied down. The wind knocked James Lindley into a banister and he fell to the ground; three times he got up, and three times the wind blew him back down. Finally he stayed down and tried to crawl. Debris shot around like bullets. As Elmer Kressberg crawled in front of Lindley, a flying two-by-four impaled him. Fighting the blowing rain, Lindley grabbed Kressberg, dragged him the rest of the way to the railroad track, and hung onto a rail.

<hr>

At about four-thirty, Edward A. Buckinger of Camp 3 had trudged step by step against the storm's fury to Carson Bradford's store, where he helped Bradford nail up some boards flapping around on the store's exterior—a job that took a long time in the growing wind. After they had done the best they could, he and Bradford went inside, and were soon joined by others who scrambled there for safety after the camp's mess tent collapsed. But even a wooden building couldn't stand against the hurricane. The store's ceiling dropped on one end and lifted on the other, and while the men scrambled out, the entire roof was torn off and tumbled into the dark sky. Then a wall blew away. As he got through the door, first-aid technician Gay Marion Postell was hit in the back of the head by the filling station pump. Everything went black.

"[When] I got outside [Bradford's], why the rest of it went away," Buckinger said later, still astonished at the memory. He made his way across the railroad tracks to the slip and boarded the *Monroe County*. Andrew J. Pfister, from Long Island City, New York, also climbed aboard. The upper deck started cracking, and Buckinger went down below, in the hull. The deck collapsed, but the hull held together.

Those who could started running for their lives. Thomas Lannon headed for the railroad tracks and lay down next to them with three others. The railroad bed was the highest ground in camp, and the rails gave some slight shelter from the wind. A nearby telephone pole threatened to fall over. "[Well], we thought that was charged with electricity, and we didn't want to get electrocuted," he said, "so we gets up out of there, went to stand up; and the shack started coming over, so we had to lay down again; it was either get your head knocked off by a little shack, or get electrocuted; so we said we would take a chance on getting electrocuted, but it happened to be there was no electricity in the wires."

Men from all three camps would tell of the sand blasting them, of having to guard their faces from it. A few also witnessed an unusual phenomenon: small sparks in the air caused by grains of sand slamming into one another. But despite obliterating the work camps, the wind wasn't the worst part of the storm. For the men caught in it, the worst part would be what they called "the tidal wave," the storm surge—the dome of water formed by the lower air pressure beneath a storm, especially a hurricane.

In a hurricane, the highest part of a storm surge accompanies the eye's leading right-hand quadrant, where the wind speed is greatest. In a Category 5 hurricane, the surge reaches 18 feet or more, and huge waves crest on top of it. A surge always achieves its greatest height in shallow water, like that surrounding the Keys, because the water has no place else to go. As the Conchs had warned more than thirty years earlier, the railroad's bed formed a nearly bridgeless rampart throughout the Upper Keys, holding back the water while the hurricane shoved in more from the Atlantic. Men who couldn't hold onto something would begin to wash away.

The surge that was now beginning brought with it driftwood and beams, which slammed into people fighting for their lives. One cubic yard of water weighs 1,700 pounds, making a big wave a powerful force, strong enough to toss James Morrison of Camp 1 atop a seven-foot-tall pile of lumber while a two-by-four slammed into his knee and another beam hit him in the head. And then, as with Gay Marion

Postell, hit in the back of the head by a filling station pump, everything went dark for Morrison.

De Forrest Rumage, an ex–Army Flying Corps soldier from Cleveland, was out in the open about 50 feet from the mess tent at Camp 3 when the roof went. Crawling on his stomach to the nearby mangrove swamp, Rumage wrapped his arms around a tree and rode it up and down with the waves, keeping his head above water. But debris carried by the wind slammed into his back. "[It] seemed to paralyze me for a second," he said. "I almost lost my grip but I hung on." He couldn't remember much after that.

As for Sain, the wind blew him through Davis's private dining quarters into a field office and through the mess hall's outer wall. He grabbed the wall and somehow avoided flying debris and mess equipment. But the water rose, lifting the floor off the foundation and pinning his right foot between two timbers. In seconds he was completely submerged. Reaching for a two-by-four, Sain used it as a lever to break free. "The only injury I received was a bruised knee, a mean cut half through the calf of my leg, and a badly sprained ankle," he reported. "No fractures of the bone."

Colonel Sheeran's secretary, Arthur Mewshaw, huddled inside his shack with four others, listening to the lumber slamming against the other shacks. "The wind, sand, and rain became so violent that it turned our shack over completely," he said. It tumbled until it hit another shack and ended upside down. Mewshaw tore out the screen window and looked around outside. He led the rest through the top and started swimming toward a tree for shelter.

Joseph Wojtkiewicz and a Camp 3 buddy pulled one man from the debris and set him on the railroad track, then they picked up another man with a broken back and also put him on the track. Captain Davis made his way by and told them to move the men to the water tank. "[And] we wasn't there five minutes, to tell the truth, not even five minutes, when the water come up," Wojtkiewicz said. "Wasn't three minutes until the whole track just raised right up against the water tank." Wojtkiewicz was on the side of the rising track, which tried to pin him against the tank. He leaped off the car and into the water. A loose tie smacked into him, but he grabbed onto a hand brake and held fast.

W. H. Chambers held onto the tank car for dear life, but the water rose 10 to 12 feet on the tank car and his grip failed. "I was swept back about one hundred yards in the brush," he said, "and how I was saved I don't know."

To Worcester, Massachusetts, native Gus Linawik at Camp 5, the storm sounded "like big machinery going around, the wind was blowing so hard." His shack shook and pulled out the nails holding it together.

His fellow veterans at Camp 5 decided almost as one to abandon their shacks, and all of them seemed to think of the cesspool nearby. One at a time, with water pouring on them, they scrambled down the two-foot-square hatch into the darkness. If they had been less than five feet tall, they could have stood. About thirty men crammed inside. Seawater poured in from a pipe running into the Atlantic, and the men on that side packed blankets and coats into the pipe to keep the water out. But the ocean kept pushing back, and when it finally won, the water quickly rose around them. They all scrambled back out. Now the wind blew so hard that the veterans started flying off into the storm. Linawik hung onto a pair of men who in turn held onto the cesspool hatch. Shacks blew past them and fluttered off in the air. A palmetto tree about 20 feet long floated by on the rising sea, and the three grabbed it and held on tight.

Forty-six-year-old Arbie Hytte of Lexington, Tennessee, and two buddies who'd also sought shelter in the cesspool found a tree and climbed to the top to keep their heads above water. Most of the others went for the tracks—the highest point in camp. "After that I don't know what happened," Hytte said. "All I could hear was fellows hollering, begging for help and praying. We couldn't help them."

In his shack at Camp 1, Raleigh LePreux, from Washington, D.C., saw the roof blow off the supply hut, and then his own shack started creaking in the wind and rain. "[We] could see these big washtubs flying through the air, then my shack started to crack a little bit," he said. LePreux leaned against the wall, but it lifted off the ground, so he fell to the floor and tried crawling outside. "[A]s soon as you started to crawl, the wind would turn you over," he said. He and two others made it to the camp flagpole, which was anchored to the ground by concrete, and LePreux held onto it with both arms. "Of course, the rest of my body was sticking right out in the open and large rocks were coming down the road and they hit me in the ribs," he recalled.

When the wind worked the flagpole loose, LePreux and the others crawled toward the railroad tracks. Suddenly he found himself alone. The storm surge swept over him and he felt himself drowning, yet managed to make it to the privately owned quarry near the camp, where he cowered behind a boulder in three feet of water. Fortunately, this quarry was higher in elevation than the one the veterans had been using on Plantation Key, across the Snake Creek Bridge.

The long-awaited train reached Windley Key at about 6:30 P.M. It chugged toward the hospital, and the refugees inside could just make out its weak headlamp. But it kept on rolling past. Everyone was shocked, but Dr. Alexander told them to be patient. "[The train] will go down to 3 and pick up 3 and 5 and then pick us up," he explained. "[And] we will all just stay here until the train comes back."

The flimsy lodge-turned-hospital was built on the lowest part of the Key. With the wind growing ever stronger, the first floor began flooding, until the water reached waist high. The deputy and Dr. Main yelled for everyone to climb to the second floor. "Dr. Alexander broke windows on one side," said Patrick Howard, "and I broke windows on the other side." They figured that would let the wind blow through instead of blowing the hospital over. Howard climbed the stairs to the second floor, leaving Dr. Main at the front door up to his belt in water. Camp 1 mail orderly Berkley Taylor stood by the rear door, also in water up to his waist. Just as Howard reached the second floor, the roof blew off, and then the entire hospital collapsed. "I was washed out by the tide to a spot near the infirmary," Taylor said. Frenchy Fecteau and Dr. Alexander leaped through the same window. "[And] of course we were separated," Fecteau said.

Inside, Albert Earl Christie saw Ben Van Ness trying to reach one of his daughters. "He was outside trying to get her," Christie said. "That was the last I saw of her." Christie was knocked unconscious, and when he came to later, he found himself clinging to a little girl. Later that night she told him her name was Frances.

Infirmary worker Willard Parker was inside too. Floating along with the surge, Parker had to unbuckle his belt and use it to strap himself to a raft. Fastened to that belt, he later testified, was a package with his important papers and his money, $5,000 in cash. All of it was swept away.

At 5:00 P.M., William W. Terry, who, like Parker, worked in the Camp 1 infirmary about half a block from the hospital, stood watching the storm build from the door of his shack. He noticed one end of the supply room begin to collapse. "The storm kept getting worse and worse and the trees around my shack began popping," he said. It grew darker, and the wind picked up even more. Terry looked past the lumber that was once the hospital at a new shack where the hospital workers slept, and the wind picked it up and whirled it through the air.

"I thought to myself, 'This won't do at all,'" Terry said. He fought his way to what he called a "little low house," where a few men stood in up to three feet of water. But another vet grabbed him and took him to a small house where five men were already sheltered.

Close by in the storm, Joe F. Honor and two men whom he knew only as Higgins and Gallagher stumbled into the Camp 1 mess together. Jackson Huffman was there, still waiting to load two tubs of dishes on the train as per Captain Hardaker's orders. With the wind now shrieking, Hardaker yelled for everyone to get out of the tent.

"[Just] then there was a crash in the mess hall and they all ran off," Honor said. "Then all of a sudden it broke and the tidal wave came in and my shack started floating around. We decided we better take a little walk." The shack next door rose up, crashed into his shack, and split it in two. Higgins and Gallagher disappeared; Honor grabbed the door and got pulled out by the sea. Huffman grabbed the cookstove. "I thought that was about the safest place in the mess hall," he said. Once the stove started giving way, a mechanic dragged Honor outside and to a washroom next door. The two could just make out the train's whistle, and decided the wind and rain were too strong to make it to the tracks—that their only chance was to wait until it let up.

Waiter Ray E. Layman ran out of the tent and made it as far as he could—just across the road that ran in front of it—when something hit him from behind. He crumpled on the spot, his back broken.

The tidal wave struck while Wilbur B. Cawthon, who worked for the *Key Veteran News*, was inside one of the cabins near the waterline by Camp 1. It pushed the cabin west. "The water began to fill in very fast," he said. Just when he had almost lost hope, another wave washed him back onto solid ground. Cawthon crawled out, pulling himself along by whatever he could grab. "I was struck by two timbers at the time, but I managed to pull my arm out from between them," he said. The timbers broke his arm and crushed his ribs. "Following that, I was struck with rocks, etc., from time to time until I reached the top of the hill and the road," he said. And then he blacked out.

John T. Clifford found himself immersed in water and trying to hold up another vet, Frank Jefferies. "I had him out there with me in the water all night," he said. "I couldn't hold him up any longer; but I brought his body on up to the road and put a card in his pocket with his name on it and his paycheck number and where his brother lived in Canton, Ohio."

John A. Conway was suddenly lying on his stomach with two other men, clinging to a telephone pole. "Something just bounded off my back," he said. He didn't know it then, but that something had crushed his spine in three places. When the water rushed over him, the others held his head above it and kept him from drowning.

Cook Grover Raines had his gear packed up and looked out of his shack at a rock fence, but thought the wind was blowing too hard to make it. He stayed in his shack until another shack blew off and almost struck his own, at which point he sought shelter in an alley between the kitchen and another building. It grew dark. He was lying about 200 feet from the tracks when the train backed past, and he could see its headlight and hear the whistle blowing.

George Joseph Senison, thirty-nine, was also waiting in his Camp 1 shack, along with his three roommates, when the walls started shaking harder and things began falling and hitting the floor. He looked out the door in time to see the roof blow off the mess tent and men running for the train that, to their astonishment, kept right on backing up. He and his roommates quickly abandoned the shack, but as soon as they got out the door, seawater rose up to their waists. "We could not face the wind—it was too strong—we had to go around the shack," he said. They grabbed one another and leaned against the shack for protection. "I heard William Clark holler that the roof was coming down," he added. "We all started away in the same direction and the roof came down on us. It must have hit every one of us."

Pinned beneath it, Senison heard the others groaning, but it was the last sound they ever made. Dragged underwater, he fought against the roof that was pressed against his back; every time he nearly broke free, the roof pushed him down again. "Finally I got hold of a beam that was drifting around with the wreckage," he remembered. "I held onto that and another beam came around and I was caught between them." The beam slammed into him, snapping a hip and breaking his pelvis. He managed to grab part of another roof and held on; it washed up against some brush and trees and stayed there, and so did Senison.

The mess tent blowing apart was enough for Clyde Brannon; he left and fought his way through the rain to the privately owned rock quarry. Many veterans were already there, and more were on their way. At about 6:45 eight veterans watched a derrick boom swerve and buckle. Its guy wires draped across the telephone lines and the arm settled above the tracks.

"If that train comes down and don't see that," William Hellman shouted, "there is going to be a wreck here, and none of us will get out."

CHAPTER EIGHT

Monday
September 2, 1935
Evening and Night

With the water continuing to rise, the train slowed to five miles per hour just before reaching Camp 1. As it did, Guy Prentiss jumped on, climbed to the top of a car, and stuck one leg through the transom. "I thought everyone on the train was drowned," he said, "the water was so high— it was shoulder deep when I climbed up. After a while I heard people talking and looked down and saw a crowd of them were there and I called to them and they broke out around the transom and got me down."

The rain was blowing hard enough to topple several telephone poles onto the passenger cars. A few people watching the train estimated the wind speed at 100 miles per hour, but

Colonel Sheeran had noted stronger gusts near Camp 3, 10 miles southwest, an hour earlier.

While the train endured the pole assault, the engine continued dragging its cars past the rock quarry near Camp 1. Suddenly the engineer hit the brakes, and the passengers lurched in their seats. William Johns, of the *Miami Daily News*, peered out through a rain-streaked window and could just make out a large cable draped between the last two passenger cars. Thinking the wire was electrified, he bolted from that car and ran into the next one forward. But the brakeman there told him a derrick from the quarry had blown over and what he had seen was a three-quarter-inch support cable.

Cook Grover Raines was lying just 200 feet from the train, yet he couldn't tell it had stopped. But a few of the men still sheltered by the quarry saw the headlight on Old 447, and one of them yelled, "Let's run for the train!" They stumbled and fell over one another as they fought the sandy wind and rain to get there. Eleven of them made it, the only men from Camp 1 to board. Also making it to the train were the wife and three young sons of Charles Cale, who operated the quarry and lived at its entrance.

Mallie K. Pitman crawled on top of the train and inspected the cable. "Yes, it was tangled pretty badly," he said, "wrapped around and everything." The cable was loose on one end, so Pitman, Conductor Gamble, and a veteran named Gottlieb straightened it out and pulled, and then other veterans grabbed on and pulled the rest of it from between the cars. All the veterans who helped with the cable boarded

the train, but the crew seemed to regard them more as potential troublemakers than refugees from an incipient disaster. "I talked to one man and he said if we didn't sit down
he would shoot us," Gottlieb said.

Guy Prentiss witnessed the same hostility from the train
crew: "Trainmaster Branch was aboard with a .35 and com-
pelled four or five of the men to help with the cable—that is
veterans, I mean. . . . [The train crew was] very cautious
about what they said, how they said it and to whom they said
it. So if anyone had a personal chat with any of the railroad
men, I do not know who, and I did not see it. I was watching the game pretty closely. I would venture to say that there
wasn't a man on the train besides a newspaper reporter that
talked with any man on the train crew."

He was referring to William Johns, who was peering
through the window while the train remained stopped by the
cable. Johns could just make out a little house less than 50
feet from the train. A couple of the Model A vets saw it too.
Wrapping his coat around his body, Johns hopped off, followed by the Model A vets, and crawled toward the cabin.
A family of seven crouched inside, ranging from grandpar-
ents down to a six-month-old baby. They were Russells,
members of a ubiquitous Upper Keys clan, and they were
soaked and cold. The wind was rocking their house. Johns
and the vets had to lie on the ground and form a human
chain to pull the family to the train.

At 7:00 P.M. on Long Key, weather observer J. E. Duane
was huddled with several others in the fishing camp's main

lodge, his own home having been destroyed. The barometer had plummeted to 27.78, and the wind was 130 miles per hour. The lodge itself had begun to disintegrate under the assault of flying timbers. Water piling up from Florida Bay to the north had now reached the railroad track.

Forty minutes after stopping near Camp 1 to untangle the cable, the train got underway again for Islamorada, two miles away. As the engine backed past them, its light glowing weakly in the dark and the rain, men crowded around the tracks tried desperately to get it to stop. Someone even threw a stone and broke a window, but the train kept on going.

Ray Sheldon had been waiting at the Islamorada train station with Deputy Sheriff Maloney, chief project auditor D. A. Malcolm, and night watchman Olin Perdue since before five-thirty, during which time the wind had rapidly increased from 70 to 100 miles per hour, then grew stronger still. At 7:00 P.M. the train station began to give way, and thirteen of the men sheltering in it ran for their lives to a boxcar nearby. Drenched to the bone, the men huddled inside among 720 bags of cement and fifteen drums of oil stored there. "This isn't my fault," Sheldon kept repeating. "This isn't my fault." He looked at Malcolm. "Do you think I'm to blame?" Malcolm didn't answer.

Ed Butters had led his family from the Matecumbe Hotel, which was threatening to fly apart, at about 6:00 P.M. He packed his wife, his three kids, his father, a grandson, and Sheldon's secretary, Mrs. Fritchman, into the family car while the hurricane destroyed the hotel. Quite possibly, huddled there, Mrs. Fritchman reassessed her disdain for Sam Cutler's storm concerns of Saturday.

In Jacksonville, Weather Bureau forecasters struggled to catch up with the storm. They had few resources; throughout the long day only one ship off the Florida coast had reported the hurricane's position. The steamship *Cerro Azul* sent its report at 6:00 P.M. to Miami, which forwarded it to Jacksonville. The teletype there was out of order, so the seven-thirty advisory went out over Western Union:

> Hoist hurricane warnings north of Key Largo to West Palm Beach and northeast storm warnings north of West Palm Beach to Titusville, and storm warnings continued elsewhere south Florida coast Titusville to Sarasota. Tropical disturbance, hurricane intensity, approaching Matecumbe Key, apparently moving north northwestward with recurving tendency. Will cause winds of about hurricane force over extreme southern Florida and strong winds over central Florida late tonight or early Tuesday morning.

But for the Matecumbe Keys, the warning was much too late.

When the relief train finally backed into the Islamorada station and stopped to pick up camp administrators, Sheldon and Perdue left the shelter of the boxcar for the engine. The wind blew Sheldon over, and he fell on ground that was wet only with rainwater. When he struggled to his feet again and started toward the engine, the water was up around his ankles. By the time he touched Old 447 the water had reached his waist. Upper Matecumbe Key was in the northern sector of the approaching storm's eye wall—the eye would pass to the south, over Lower Matecumbe Key—and here the storm surge was coming ashore. Sheldon crawled inside the cab and looked at engineer Haycraft. "You are the man we are looking for," he said with forced joviality. As Haycraft started the train rolling again toward Camp 3, Sheldon checked his watch by a light on the boiler. It was almost 8:20 P.M. The train went 100 yards, and then began breaking up.

The first sign was a lurch and the grinding of the emergency brake. Conductor J. E. Gamble heard it and started walking back through the train, checking each car to see if someone had pulled the brake. In the rear car, passengers peering through the back window saw that the last boxcar had blown off the tracks. That had set off the brake. To the passengers in the rest of the cars, though, the storm had risen to such a crescendo and rocked the cars so much that they thought the train was still moving.

The railroad bed reached seven feet above sea level, and the train's floor was five feet above that. At 8:20 P.M. a huge wave riding the storm surge slammed into the train, and the smoking car where Johns sat lifted—gently, it seemed to him—and tumbled over on its side. The sea swirled the cars around "like straws," Johns said. One by one the windows burst, spraying seawater through the cars as if from a fire hose, pressing everyone against the opposite wall. Johns grabbed a door and held tight. The car came to rest against another boxcar, and then everyone inside panicked, scrambling to the door. Johns could see that the next car was tilted even more, and that a furious stream of water rushed between the two. "Boys, go back to that smoking compartment!" he yelled. They turned around and scrambled back into the smoking car. Johns was the last one to make it inside. Huge waves continued rocking the train while rain blew in, cutting visibility to zero. "[After] I got myself quieted down I began to think if there is any way in the world I can get out of here, I want to get out," Johns recalled.

Once the car he was in stopped sliding on its side, Mallie Pitman collected himself and crawled outside into waist-high water. With the wind blowing and the waves slamming debris into everything, Pitman realized he was safer inside the train. He crawled into another car, where perhaps thirty people now stood, soaking wet and shocked. Despite what others testified later, Pitman maintained that "the water never did cover the entire car." The engine remained upright, but inside, Haycraft, Sheldon, Perdue, and the others were standing in seawater, which doused the fire in the firebox.

Less than a mile away, outside the remains of the Matecumbe Hotel, Ed Butters realized that his car could not protect his family from the rising water, so he led them onto a nearby bus parked behind a screen of mangroves, where they watched the water rise around them.

In the house off Camp 1 where William Terry hid out with five other veterans, a wave hit and rolled the structure three or four times. Once the house stopped rolling, Terry got out and saw houses collapsing all around him. "[The] water was so severe and you could not stand up; the wind blowed so hard you could not stand without holding onto something," he explained. That's exactly what he did: he grabbed a nearby house, but the siding came off and slammed into him, pinning him by the chest and stomach. "I was down under that thing straining and trying to get out from under the water which went over my head," he said. "I thought I was gone."

Jacob Herbert of Camp 1 estimated that by eight-thirty his shack was picked up by water. "[And] all of a sudden *crash*," he said. "The only thing I remember is that a blanket and a mattress fell over my shoulders—it probably saved my life. I heard a crash and felt my head—then I felt myself fading away, like soaring into space, floating, floating." When he came to he was vomiting, pinned down by lumber.

Frenchy Fecteau, a poor swimmer, was washed over the quarry and into a grove of trees. His pocket watch stopped at 8:23.

The only building made from concrete in the Upper Keys was in Tavernier, four and a half miles northeast of Camp 1 and six miles northeast of Islamorada. It was the picture show, the Cinemorada Theater, but unfortunately it was still under construction. Some of the town's residents may have headed for it, but more took shelter in railroad boxcars. About four or five veterans were in the Tavernier jail, but the sheriff let them out when conditions got bad. Miscreants, perhaps, but no fools, they too made a beeline for shelter. So did four or five other vets caught out in the open. Everyone in Tavernier survived.

At Islamorada's Pioneer Cemetery, the angel standing guard over the grave of Etta Delores Pinder toppled and broke. The left wing flew nearly a mile west, landing in the middle of the highway.

———— ∞∞∞ ————

After bolting from the Camp 1 mess tent early in the storm, John W. Sipes had fought the wind to his shack and "stayed there a little bit, and by that time it kept getting worse and shaking the buildings; so I didn't take nothing out with me." He ran back toward the mess, which by then had blown away along with the canteen. Dead and wounded littered the camp, reminding him of the trenches during the war. Seeing an injured man lying on the ground across the street, Sipes ran over. All he could do for the man was to get him a blanket. "I am going to leave here," he told the vet. "I am going to the rock quarry, I believe it is the safest place right now." But the man refused to come along, so Sipes left him lying there and crawled down into the quarry, which was seven to nine feet deep and offered good shelter. The wind blew a toolbox off the ledge and nearly cracked him on the skull, after which he crawled over to a corner to avoid more blowing debris. There, he came across a couple of men he knew.

"Well, the train ain't a-coming," one said shortly after 6:30 P.M. "We just as well stay here for the rest of the night. This is the safest place we can get." Just then Sipes heard the train's whistle blow, but the hurricane obscured it from view, and after it passed he couldn't hear it at all. They figured it was going down to Camp 3 and coming back up, so they tried to run for the tracks and catch it on its way back. "[We] all made a run to go over there to the track, and I got blowed about 50 feet right on my head," he said. "So that settled the train." He grabbed a boulder and held on. The storm was so dark and violent that Sipes lost sight of the men he'd made the run with. But then he stepped on one man's feet. "[He] jumped up and commenced hollering . . . so I said to him then, 'You boys shouldn't be sleeping here this hour of the night, you might all be killed.' " After that attempt at humor, it got eerily calm, then the wind reversed course. This may have been the northernmost extremity of the eye brushing past; if so, the time must have been later than Sipes thought, closer to 8:30.

Sipes changed positions on the rock. "[I] stayed there probably thirty minutes," he said, "and never seen no train." The others laid down and covered themselves with blankets, but after a few minutes a wave swept in. Sipes tried to grab one of the men, but the wind and water seemed to carry him away. "He said he was in two feet of us," Sipes recalled, "but I never seen him no more that night."

Men on Lower Matecumbe Key who had never lived through a hurricane, who had no concept of one, told of two storms. The first blew in from the Gulf, shrieking northerly blasts preceding the eye. Then came a pause of perhaps forty minutes, and then the second storm blew in from the south, from the ocean. The veterans couldn't know it, but they were living through the hurricane's eye. This eye was unusually tight. While the average hurricane has a 20-mile-diameter eye, modern estimates of the Labor Day Hurricane's eye diameter are between 8 and 10 miles. The high winds in the eye wall created a centrifugal effect in the narrow eye: the night sky above was cloudless, clear as glass, idyllic.

Sometime between 8:00 and 9:00 P.M. the wind over the Alligator Reef Lighthouse, five miles east and south of Camp 5 and seven and a half miles due east of Camp 3, dropped briefly from the northeast, then roared in from the southeast as the northern edge of the hurricane's eye brushed past. The lighthouse keepers were terrified but still alive. At almost the same time, the eye's leading edge was making landfall on Lower Matecumbe Key.

"[It] quieted down just like that, just stopped," said James

B. Lindley of Camp 3, "and the stars come up and the wind seemed to get warm, and it was just as still, a piece of paper wouldn't flutter in the air." The group of veterans around him had been holding onto the railroad tracks out in the open. A fisherman named Smitty walked past and told them, "Boys, find a place. This is right in the middle of it, and it will be right back." Smitty also advised them to move out of the way of a pile of loose lumber to a spot a half mile from their camp—right at the water tank car. They joined the others already holding on there.

Colonel Sheeran and about thirty other men—mostly fishermen and civilian employees who had elected to stay with the equipment—were still sheltering inside the houseboat *Sarasota* in Hurricane Creek. "We had more on than was safe as it was," he recalled. During the eye, Arthur Mewshaw tried swimming and wading to get within shouting distance. Sheeran hollered back that the storm was not yet over, that Mewshaw and the others needed to find shelter on high ground while they had the opportunity. Mewshaw also sought out the tank car.

During the first part of the storm, William Thompson of Camp 5 had taken shelter among the shacks with Eugene Cunningham. Then the wind plunged a splinter into Thompson's back. He lay on the ground until someone—he didn't know who—helped him up and to the water tank car, where someone else—again, he didn't know who—pulled the splinter out.

The surge from the Gulf side that preceded the eye had been bad, but those same northerly winds had held the Atlantic at bay. When the eye was over Camp 5, a supply sergeant set a chest of smokes on top of the car. "If it does come," he said, "we will have cigarettes." A little boy, obviously terrified, asked Cunningham what he was going to do, and Cunningham said he didn't know, that they would all have to do the best they could for themselves. Just before the second wall of water hit, Cunningham put his left arm around the boy. They could hear the oncoming roar, and when it arrived, the wave swept the supply sergeant off the car along with his cigarettes, but somehow Cunningham maintained a grip on the tank car with his right hand and held onto the little boy while grabbing the hair of another veteran with his left hand. With superhuman strength he heaved the man—by the hair—on top of the car. Others grabbed Cunningham and pulled him and the boy up.

Now, with the eye's passage, the ocean rushed back in, low pressure combining with southerly blasts and seas that may have topped 100 feet outside the reefs to overwhelm the low-lying Keys. When the tidal wave hit, Thompson was holding onto the second or third rung of the tank car. The water came up to his chest, but he held on there the rest of the night.

J. W. Taylor stayed in his Camp 3 shack until the eye

passed overhead, then wrapped his head in a blanket and waded out into waist-deep water on his way to the railroad. A man grabbed him by the hand and led him to the ferry-boat, which had been shoved from its slip up onto the railroad embankment. He estimated that twenty or thirty men were on board, and that it could have held between seventy and eighty. The vets wanted to stay on board, but Captain Albury told them, "You men had better leave the boat because this storm is getting worse and this ship won't be safe."

Only a few followed Albury out. Taylor helped lash the ferry to the railroad track, and then men emerged from its innards and said, "Boys, we can hear it coming." Everyone fled down into the engine room. "When the tidal wave came over," Taylor said, "the boat came up like it was going to turn over, but it didn't bother us very much"—not even when an ammonia tank exploded next to Andrew J. Pfister's head and seawater rose up to the veterans' necks. They were staying put.

Leaving the ferry, Captain Albury and his engineer, Lewis Crews, headed toward the Camp 3 ambulance. But when the wave hit, the ambulance washed out into the sea, and Crews drowned. Albury managed to grab a piece of driftwood, and held on for the better part of an hour before landing on an embankment, which he clung to for the rest of the night.

As the eye crossed Lower Matecumbe, Davis and some of his men from Camp 3 gathered and "decided that the beer boat and ferryboat in front of camp and the Panama dredge boat in back of camp could hold some," he said. As for

Davis, "I was going to the water tank car . . . and try and ride the storm in the open, and each man chose whichever place he wanted as it was now just every one for himself."

"[We] could hear, twenty minutes before the wind hit, we could hear that roar," James Lindley said. "[I]t began to roar in your ears just like a faraway rumble, that wind and water, and the water when it come over [the reef] just like that, and we began to mount the car."

Seventy to 100 men sought shelter on the tank car. "It started coming in over the reef, and we watched it coming in, and it looked like white foam," Davis said. A wall of water at least 25 feet high slammed into them and washed some off, and the wind blew more off, and then the car began tipping over and others leaped rather than be squashed under its weight. Those moments, Davis figured later, brought the biggest loss of life to Camp 3. The wave washed out the railroad. "It was all a person could do to hold on," he said. Just before the car tipped completely, the main railroad track fell against it and propped the car upright.

"When this tidal wave came," said Earle Roach, "all of us grabbed a good hold of the tank. . . . The fellow alongside of me was washed off."

Arthur Mewshaw was also swept away. "I approximate the time that the wave picked me up at about nine-ten," he said, "because all the watches of the boys who were drowned stopped at such hour." While fighting to keep his head above water, Mewshaw took hold of a telephone wire, which broke, and then grabbed a limb, which also broke. A second limb, however, held.

While most of the Camp 3 shacks had already either blown off or washed away, "mine happened to stand till about the last," Albert Thilmann said. Once the wind took it, water flowed up to his waist. He and another man behind him set out for the railroad track and the water tank. The man began going under, and Thilmann tried to help lift his head above water. Then an object struck Thilmann and pinned him against the tank car. "I guess that is when I was unconscious," he said. "I went over backwards and hung there the rest of the night."

When Gay Marion Postell came to after being whacked in the head by a gas pump, he was inside a car and the eye was passing over. Someone inside told him that the ambulance driver was seriously hurt and asked Postell, a first-aid specialist, if he could do anything for him. Still woozy, Postell got out and inspected Elmer Kressberg. The length of two-by-four stuck out of his side, and he begged to go to the hospital. Postell tried to pull the beam out, but it wouldn't budge, so he gave Kressberg a dose of paraldehyde, a painkiller, and asked some of the men to help carry him to the ambulance. But one of the shacks had rolled over on it, and the ambulance wasn't going anywhere anyway, not with the roads underwater. The men put Kressberg on a stretcher and carried him to a truck, loaded him in the back, and pointed the truck toward the wind. Then everyone scattered for the tank car.

Postell got there just as the tidal wave hit, and there was no space left on top. "I grabbed hold of the rail on the side and pretty soon something crashed me and everything else take away," he said. "I landed in a bush and stayed there till morning, three hundred yards away."

⸺ ∞ ⸺

On Long Key, in the eye's southern sector, J. E. Duane reported a fifty-five-minute lull beginning about nine-twenty, during which stars shone brightly in a clear sky to the north. In the midst of this lull the sea rose rapidly. "I put my flashlight out on the sea," Duane wrote, "and could see walls of water which seemed many feet high." The storm surge that had arrived an hour earlier on Lower Matecumbe Key, in the dangerous semicircle of the advancing eye, was now inundating Long Key as well.

Duane retreated to the Key's last standing house, where the island's few other residents were also sheltering. By the time he covered the 60 feet to the door, the water was waist deep. As he waded inside, the house floated from its foundation. At 10:10 P.M. his barometer had dropped to 27.02 inches and the wind was returning, this time from the south-southwest. Five minutes later the wind was howling again—stronger, Duane thought, than at any previous point in the evening—and the house began to break up. He got one last look at his barometer as the house disintegrated around him, reading 26.98 inches, then dropped it into the water "and was blown outside into the sea; got hung up in broken fronds of coconut tree and hung on for dear life. I was then struck by some object and knocked unconscious."

On nearby Craig Key, less than two miles from Camp 3, a man named Ivar Olson survived the storm in his small boat nestled in the mangroves. As the eye passed by, the pressure dropped far below what Olson's barometer could measure, but he kept scratching marks on the brass frame so he could see when the pressure stopped falling. When Weather Bureau meteorologists tested the barometer later, they found it to have been in fine working order. Calibrating Olson's scratches, the meteorologists determined that the lowest read 26.35—the lowest barometric pressure of the twentieth century, and maybe in all of history.

Safely north of the hurricane, the men in Dr. Main's car— Cash, Walter Smith, the veteran Legaras, and Roy Hurley— reached Miami. "We monkeyed around town for a little while, then we went to the depot to wait for the [relief] train." They reached the depot at around 9:00 P.M. "[First] thing we learned was that all communication was out from Homestead south," said Hurley.

No one in the outside world knew what cataclysm had been unleashed down there.

CHAPTER NINE

Tuesday
September 3, 1935

Before midnight Monday, Fred Ghent finally reached Hollywood from Jacksonville in his freshly oiled car and found Sam Cutler there, waiting for the relief train. They waited together. When it still hadn't arrived by midnight, the two went on to the Miami depot seeking more information, arriving there at nearly 1:00 A.M. The train wasn't there either, and there was no news of it.

At the station, Ghent and Cutler ran into Frederick Snyder, who ran the Camp 1 canteen, and the vet whom Snyder knew only as "the little fellow." The two had made it into Miami in Hardaker's pickup truck—despite a short flooded stretch north of Homestead—and waited for two or three hours or more in Miami's train station for the relief train to appear. Ghent asked them why they were hanging around there. Return to Homestead, he ordered them, and left to drive there himself. So Snyder and his companion got back into Hardaker's truck and drove down.

"When we reached Homestead, we started looking for the train," Snyder said, "figuring it had come into Homestead and was on a siding, but we could not see it." And though Ghent had left Miami before them and was already supposed to be there, they couldn't find him either. They checked the fire station, but no one there had seen him; someone told them Ghent was in the train station, but no one saw him there. Finally they found him in his car, lying down. They couldn't tell if he was asleep but didn't want to bother him. Besides, it was pouring and they were soaked. Snyder went back inside the station and fell asleep on the floor, exhausted.

Roy Hurley, one of the men who had driven away from the Snake Creek Hospital in Dr. Main's car, stayed around the Miami train depot from 9:00 P.M. until 2:00 A.M. without hearing a word from the camps. No relief train arrived. He saw no veterans, no leaders, no equipment, nothing. Hurley and his companions split up to stay in different hotels.

At daybreak Ghent, Cutler, Eugene Pattison (who had driven his pickup out with a load of Camp 1 vets the day before), and E. W. Nabal, the Camp 1 first sergeant, rose, drank coffee, and started driving down to the Keys. Ghent and Cutler were in Ghent's car, Pattison and Nabal in Pattison's truck, and Snyder and the little fellow in Hardaker's pickup. The caravan reached Snake Creek by 6:30 A.M., where they found the bridge blown away. "[Even] though I could not get across I could see that the entire camp [Camp 1] was gone," Nabal said.

While Ghent and Pattison stayed at Snake Creek, one man asked Snyder if he could pull-start another truck that was needed to take an injured woman to the hospital. The truck was in Tavernier, about six miles north of Snake Creek. Along the way they met up with a man who said he had a surefire way to breach the gap across Snake Creek: toss a spool of cable in the back of the truck, take it back down to Snake Creek, and have someone swim an end of it across. Snyder rejected his plan outright; the current was simply too swift for anyone to swim across, much less while dragging a cable. "There didn't seem to be anything else to do," Snyder said, "so we went back to [Tavernier] and helped some people get to Homestead."

When Roy Hurley got up in his hotel room at six-thirty Tuesday morning, there was still no news from below Homestead. Returning to the Miami depot, he boarded the 7:20 A.M. local train to Key West and waited for it to pull out of the station—and waited. He heard no news about the delayed departure until a railroad employee finally walked through the cars to tell the passengers that the train's departure had been postponed indefinitely due to washouts. That was all he said.

"That was the first actual news that told me that there was something wrong down there," Hurley said. He got off the train with a nurse named Miss McCloud and a hairdresser, Miss Miller, and they walked together to a filling station nearby. "[And], being lucky, we happened to meet a young fellow that had put in sound equipment at the picture show at Tavernier," Hurley explained, "and he said he was going down there." They all piled into the man's car. On the way to Homestead, Hurley saw no indication of anything more than strong wind. From Homestead to Key Largo he noticed a tree or two blown over, nothing more. But as they neared Tavernier he saw barns toppled—some split in half. "We entered Tavernier," he said, and "it seemed as though every house in Tavernier was blown in one spot; they weren't smashed up so much, they were lifted bodily." It must have been a tidal wave, he figured. From there to Snake Creek, every house was blown over. The landscape was simply scoured.

Two miles above Snake Creek, he saw three bodies alongside the tracks; one lay on the track itself. According to Hurley, they were "blowed up the size of [silent-film comedian] Fatty Arbuckle." Just a half mile from Snake Creek, near the garage and the Plantation Key quarry, the camp trucks lay on their sides. He figured about 120 feet of the railroad bridge was washed out. Snake Creek itself had broadened to some 60 to 70 feet wide, and its normally swift current rushed by even faster than usual. "I tried to talk to two men across the gap, but the wind was blowing pretty hard and you couldn't hear what they were saying," he reported. But motioning through signs, the two indicated that they counted 78 dead and 30 injured in Camp 1.

Pelted by rain and by a wind that was still blowing at 50 miles per hour, Hurley's group started back north just as

Monroe County sheriffs cordoned off the area. "And by the time we got in Miami then the place was practically under martial law," he said, "and they wouldn't let us go back down, although we volunteered to go back down and identify the dead." Instead, the National Guard, Miami's American Legion Harvey W. Seeds Post 29, and the local CCC contingent went down. "[I] don't see how in the dickens they ever expected to identify anybody with the ones they took down there that they did," Hurley said. But Governor David Sholtz wasn't worried about identifying the bodies; he sent the National Guard to prevent looting. At the same time, National Guard troops in Key West were mobilizing to approach the Upper Keys from the south.

Eugene Lowkis, who had spent the night at the railroad station in Miami, and Mr. Wright, the camps' purchasing agent, also made it to Snake Creek in the morning. There they found Ghent and Cutler. "Do you think there's many killed over there?" Lowkis overheard someone ask Ghent. "I don't think so," Ghent told him. (That evening Ghent repeated the line to an Associated Press reporter.)

A man whom Lowkis knew only as Mr. Johnson stood on the far side, signaling to the men, but none of them could make out what he said. To Lowkis, Johnson seemed in a daze. Lowkis went as far as he could to the end of the railroad trestle and tried to signal that help was coming. Nabal and Wright volunteered to swim across, but when they entered the water the current nearly swept them away. Nabal, though, made it across on the first boat, sometime between 9:30 or 10:00 A.M., along with a man representing an undertakers' association. One of the first bodies he saw was Dr. Main's.

⊶⊷

By midnight Monday the core of the hurricane had passed over the Upper Keys and was crossing Florida Bay. At 2 A.M. it slammed Cape Sable, scouring it to ground level and devastating the coastal village of Flamingo. In its wake in the Upper Keys it left slowly climbing barometers, winds that were still too strong for a man to stand in, bone-chilling rain, and a scene of utter desolation.

All through Monday night and on into Tuesday morning the men caught in the mangroves at Camp 3 called out to one another to see how many still lived. For the men clinging to the water tank car it was a different story. "This storm raged all night, and it was impossible for us to get off the tank car until daylight," said Ben Davis. At first light Davis slipped down to help three men pinned between the track and the car. Two were still alive. "We made our way around the camp and piles of wreckage and also the ground surrounding Camp 3 to rescue and relieve the injured," he said, "but due to the fact that the storm had washed our ambulance away, which was loaded with all emergency medical supplies, we had no medical attention." He and the men took shelter from the rain and wind wherever they could.

When the water receded, William W. Terry was on one of the high spots at Camp 1, virtually blinded by sand. "The reason I got my eyes in such a fix, I kept trying to look to see if I saw a house or something coming, so I could keep clear," he said. An object that had pinned him slid off, and Terry just sat, exhausted, on a big bush until around 3:00 A.M. He knew that a 10,000-gallon water tank car had been left on the camp's railroad siding the day before by the same train that had delivered the tank car to Camp 3, and he could hear people hollering from that direction. "Finally about three o'clock I could see something, some kind of an old flashlight nearly burned out," he said. The wind was still too strong for walking. "I crawled to that [light]. Had to hold to the grass, rocks, and finally made it." When he reached the car, seven or eight others had already congregated, including two women. "I got to the other side of that tank and that wind just howled and howled and kept right on till daylight and still howling," he said. By 9:00 A.M. it had weakened enough for a man to walk into it. From all directions, people made their way to the tank car, until just about everyone left alive in camp had gathered around it.

That morning, Frenchy Fecteau stirred in the quarry near Camp 1. "The only thing I had on . . . was my belt and my trousers and a bathing suit I happened to have on underneath," he said. "All of my clothes were taken right off, shoes and all." He stumbled through the rain to the water tank car and waited with the rest.

As soon as it was daylight—as soon as he could see what he was doing—Arthur Brown of Camp 3 jumped off the small bridge he'd held onto all night and swam about 30 yards across to where the railroad track used to be, and to where the Camp 3 water tank car now stood. As the camp's time-keeper, and one who was familiar with everyone there, Brown made a list of who was still living and who was dead. He counted 136 veterans alive and 36 dead, most of the latter tangled in the mangroves or bobbing in the waves. Brown wrote up a separate list of 11 Camp 5 survivors who'd made it down to Camp 3.

The storm hadn't been kind to the dead. "Some of them were pretty hard to recognize," said Edward Buckinger, "because the majority of them, in my opinion, were knocked out by timber and that before they were drowned. Most of the bodies were pretty well bled, you know, and the ones that didn't bleed, they swelled."

"I knew every one personally," said Joseph Hovranko, "but the next day you could not identify them."

Neither could John Fisher, also of Camp 3, though for a different reason; Fisher had been nearly blinded too. "[My] eyes was all bloodshot from the sand and storm," he said. "I had a towel wrapped around my eyes most all that day."

At dawn Wilton Lindsey Smith cooked up a hot breakfast for the men on the houseboat *Sarasota* and brewed them some hot coffee in order to steel their nerves for the day ahead. Then they ventured out to Camp 3 to help the wounded as best they could without first-aid supplies. After that, they started searching for the dead.

"We found the dead floating under trees," Smith said, "in trees, in the swamps, under railroad tracks." They gathered up 36 bodies and laid them out on the boat slip, but that was all they could do. According to Richard Lawrence Bow, who had spent the hurricane on the *Sarasota*, conditions still weren't safe. The low, sandy ground was covered with water, and debris floated about. "[Survivors] were more liable to injury and infection and delay in trying to work under those conditions."

De Forrest Rumage survived the night with his broken back, clinging to a mangrove tree. Early in the morning—he believed at five o'clock—the hurricane's ferocity subsided to about 40 miles per hour. "[We] just crawled into any shelter we could," he said. "There happened to be a couple of shacks wedged up end to end and that is where I put in most of the day. He received what first aid others could administer, which was very little. But his back didn't bother him too much as long as he didn't try to sit. "As long as I was on the go, it seemed that my back didn't bother me, but when I sat down that paralyzed me," he said.

After being washed off the Camp 3 tank car by a wave, Peter Donahue had swum for his life. When he found a tree big enough to hold him, he held onto it. Throughout the night he heard the boys yelling for one another. "I suffered so much from the cold," he said. After the storm subsided he returned to the tank car, where he found one corpse lying beside it and several more scattered through the woods. Along with other survivors, Donahue began picking up bodies.

A severely injured Albert Thilmann, from Washington, D.C., hung upside down all night, unconscious and pinned against the tank car. Thilmann had suffered broken ribs and had a spinal injury and a huge hole punched in his leg. The two or three vets who found him hanging there at 6:00 A.M. had to cut him out of his clothes just to get him down off the car. "When they got me, I could not talk anymore," he said. The vets laid him out on the sand, barely clothed and surrounded by the dead and dying. Among them was Elmer Kressberg, the man impaled by the two-by-four, who was still alive but just barely. "He just lay there; no one to help him," said Thilmann. To give the nearly naked Thilmann at least a little shelter, the vets re-erected one of the shacks, carried him inside, and built a fire to warm him. That's all they could do.

On board the relief train that long night, no one could say for certain whether they were on dry land—there was no *dry* land to be seen—or in the ocean. "[The] thing that scared us was we didn't know where we were," reporter William Johns said, "and we thought the whole side would slip off into the water, and the bottom fill up and be caught in there like rats in a trap." They didn't know, that is, until a flash of lightning at around 3:30 A.M. revealed that they were indeed on solid ground. "The miraculous thing," he added, "was the lights in our car never went out during the whole thing." Each car had its own battery, and when the train blew over, some batteries shorted out. Johns was in a car that stayed alight—although, as the night wore on, the lights grew dimmer; by 4:00 A.M. the battery died completely, leaving them sitting in the dark.

They stayed aboard the train until dawn, when the wind and rain died down just a bit. As they emerged, the rain picked up again, and so did the wind—Johns estimated it reached 60 miles per hour—and he and the others made their way into the first baggage car. The car leaned against the bank at a 45-degree angle, and all of them had to walk up the bottom corner to get into it. Nerves on edge from surviving the storm and from the continuing tumultuous weather, they crouched there throughout the day.

As daylight materialized over Camp 5, it revealed a scene of incomprehensible destruction. The few vets left alive— eleven of the approximately 125 who had been in the camp when the storm began—saw that everything, every building, had blown down. Gus Linawik remained up in a tree, his eyes full of sand and his ears burning from the blasting sand and the saltwater spray. At first, not knowing what was beneath him, he didn't want to climb down, but Blackey Lyons assured him that the ground was just below.

"Let's go down and rest ourselves," Lyons said, reassuring him, and so Linawik took a chance and felt around and found the ground with his toes. Lyons got down, and so did another veteran. It was still raining hard, and Linawik was tired, cold, and hungry. "My shirt was torn off by the wind and the back of my ears were sore from the waves," he said. The three managed to find the railroad tracks, which had been picked up like a rope and tossed over the road in one place, out to sea in another. There wasn't much left of Camp 5, nor were there many left alive. The long bridge connecting the Upper and Lower Matecumbe Keys had fallen and washed away, cutting off their exit north.

"Let's go down towards Camp 3," Linawik said, figuring they could at least find a boat down there—a way to get away. Walking warmed them up a little. Two more men and then four others emerged from the brush that remained, so they grew to a group of nine. They also came upon a dazed woman walking from Camp 3, trying to go north up to Camp 1. She had no shoes. Linawik and Lyons explained that the road was washed out, and she turned around and followed them south. But soon they found the sea had also washed out the road ahead. The ten turned around and headed back to Camp 5, where they found shelter behind some machinery. By 10:30 A.M. a few civilians who had lived around Camp 3 reached them. The civilians wanted to continue up to Camp 1 and send a message for help.

Linawik's group explained how deep the water was between Upper and Lower Matecumbe, but the civilians, desperate, convinced themselves they might just be able to swim across. The vets asked the civilians about the water's depth in the washout above Camp 3, and they learned that it reached up to the civilians' waists. That was nothing, so Linawik's ten got up and started south again. It was still raining and the wind was still blowing, and the woman still had no shoes. They wrapped her feet in clothes and walked the five miles. "When we got to Camp 3 the tents were tipped over, but not torn up so bad," Linawik said. "The rain and wind were not bad. We took her into a place with a bunch of canned goods.

We tried to get ourselves a drink of water or something. We found some soda water and canned goods. We put her in a tent . . . so she could rest, and the balance of us stayed around there all night."

John Skularicos, the Camp 3 veteran who had proselytized while the storm raged, went to the tank car in the morning and saw a dead man hanging there, squeezed by a pipe and turned black. He helped some others get the body down. He saw more and more dead—20 or more—but that was more than he could take. "[After] I was in the hospital about seventeen years . . . I couldn't stand to look at them kind of peoples no more," he said, "and I just laid down."

When Ray Layman of Camp 1 came to at daylight he was still holding onto a log and lying on a dead man's leg. Two other corpses were next to him. His back was broken and so were two of his ribs. Raleigh LePreux wandered around the camp and found bodies everywhere, some covered in lumber, some with holes torn in their heads from projectiles, most without any identification. Like the rest, he made his way to the water tank car, where the men built fires to warm and dry themselves and brew coffee. Injured by flying timbers, Dr. Alexander walked along the railroad track about 100 feet to his car, with the coral slicing his feet, got in, and crawled onto the rear shelf. He remained there until noon, when he crawled back out and over to the fire by the tank car. There, some vets laid him on a blanket, and he stayed until dark.

Wilbur B. Cawthon of the *Key Veteran News* crawled into the hole of what was once a building and stayed there

through the night. His right arm was broken in two places, his ribs were crushed on both sides, and his body was covered with an assortment of cuts and bruises. At dawn he worked his way out of the collapsed building and found Captain Hardaker and a group of men standing around. Hardaker had a broken arm as well, but he found a beer and offered it to Cawthon, then saw to it that Cawthon had a mattress and a blanket.

All that day the veterans waited for help to arrive. It was windy and raining hard, sure, and the waves were rough on the ocean side; but inland, from the Gulf, some veterans said it seemed possible for some rescue launch to navigate. The men in charge took it hardest. Colonel Sheeran "looked like he lost about ten pounds through worry," according to Charles King. "I never saw a man age so quickly," W. H. Chambers said about Blackie Pugh. "I bet he aged 20 years that night. He was standing there with tears running out of his eyes." And yet, despite personal hardship, they did their best to help the men.

George Senison of Camp 1 lay outside where the Snake Creek Hospital had been, where its ruins should have been but weren't, unable to move. He had a broken left hip and a broken pelvis. He called for help for two hours, but no one answered. Then he heard others around, picking through the wreckage. "I heard one fellow say, 'Let's pick up some of these boys and give their bodies halfway decent treatment.' " Senison forced himself to crawl to the road, and stayed there until noon before anyone came by. "Some of the boys were coming around there from all over. They were making a fire across the track but I could not get to it. One fellow finally got me a wet blanket and I lay there until about 6:00 P.M."

As Ira Hatcher regained consciousness inside the collapsed Snake Creek Hospital, he was screaming and veterans were digging him out from beneath piles of lumber. Once they got him out they found that Hatcher's neck was broken. He lay in place until midnight. "Nothing done for us Tuesday—didn't have a thing to eat even," Hatcher said. "Kitchen all blew away and nothing there to eat."

Charles Reginald Austin woke up in the Windley Key quarry with Dick Brady, Sam Gatta, and Andy Beganske scattered around him. During the hurricane, Austin's shack in Camp 1 had collapsed, and he and the others, along with Bill Knowles, were washed into the quarry 200 yards away. After he got his bearings, Austin went back into his shack and ran into Knowles, uninjured and walking around. As darkness fell Tuesday he went to the fire built beside the tracks at Camp 1 and stayed there, awaiting evacuation.

———— ✖✖✖ ————

When chauffeur Thomas J. Nash first heard of the hurricane, he wasn't even in the Keys, but he instantly drove down to help out his friends. At Tavernier a National Guardsman stopped him from going any farther, so he drove to the hospital and talked with the FERA supervisor there, telling her that he was the chauffeur at Headquarters and that he knew the Keys. She gave him a pass, but when the Guardsman stopped him again, the pass didn't get him through. This time, however, Nash saw a deputy sheriff he'd met on the highway project and talked the deputy into letting him pass. He got as far as the washed-out bridge at Snake Creek.

Mrs. Carson Bradford couldn't reach her husband. He owned the store at Camp 3, and she didn't know it yet, but the store had blown away. Worried sick, she chartered a small plane and rode up and down the Keys in it, searching for him. But Mrs. Bradford and the pilot saw nothing below—no camps, no hospital, no activity. Both Matecumbes were nearly submerged. She grew more distraught. They looked for some sign of the relief train, but saw only half of one car. After risking their lives in high wind and rain, the pilot talked her into giving up for the day. He flew her back to Miami, telling her they'd try again the next day.

In the late afternoon the wind and rain abated enough for reporter William Johns to walk over to what was left of the Matecumbe Hotel, looking for someone who could help him get out of there. No such luck. Most of the hotel had simply blown away. He walked back to the baggage car to spend the night.

Like Johns, a few of the Camp 1 veterans also abandoned the train and set out north to return to their camp. The road—and the railroad—had washed out. In Islamorada the church and the school were gone; the veterans didn't know it, but only 10 of the school's 65 students remained alive.

When the men reached the Whale Harbor channel separating Upper Matecumbe from Windley Key, they found it too deep and swift to wade across. Clyde Brannon and some of the Camp 1 veterans he walked with found many of the dead, whom they wrapped in blankets they found lying nearby. "That is the best we could do," he said, "because we were all in, ourselves." They too returned to the train, where they built a fire, salvaged some canned goods from the warehouse, and shared what they had with the train crew. And the crew shared some gossip with them. "[Two] or three of them was talking," Brannon said, "and they said on account of $300 not being put up for the train, delayed them from getting out of Miami to bring the train."

"I was told by a heavyset man, possibly the train conductor," George Rough said, "that the Jacksonville office refused to post the necessary funds for the train. The amount was $300." The rumor may have been baseless, but it was also persistent.

Ray Sheldon, too, left the train and trudged north, only to find the route cut off by water. Turning back, he made his way to what remained of the Matecumbe Hotel, huddling there with other survivors as night fell.

⸻

That evening on Snake Creek's north shore, someone brought down an outboard, and someone else trailered in another boat. A group of ten men from Homestead—members of the fire department—arrived at dusk and set across in the boats to rescue survivors. They worked all night, as fast as possible.

One of the first they evacuated was Arnold B. Flow, who floated across the creek at 11:30 P.M. Along with a couple of bruises and a puncture wound on his left leg, Flow had a six-inch-long stick driven below his shoulder blade and stuck against his spine. Ira Hatcher, the man with the broken neck, went across at midnight, as did Dr. Alexander. All told, some 160 veterans made it across the creek Tuesday night. "[Every] time we could get hold of an outboard motor and skiff," said J. R. Combs, a Miami native who had helped build the camps the year before, "we dragged it over and got across there."

The rescuers continued laboring into the early morning hours. And yet few people—if any—outside the Keys knew the true extent of the devastation. The Weather Bureau assured the Associated Press that the storm had not compared in size or intensity with the great hurricanes of 1926 and 1928. They were right about its size, but horribly wrong about its strength. Plowing northward off the Gulf Coast of Florida, it was still a powerful Category 4 storm.

Late Tuesday night, members of the American Legion's Harvey W. Seeds Post 29 of Miami, carrying gas lanterns, boarded a small outboard and set out on an expedition to explore the damaged areas. Crossing Snake Creek, they first stopped at a campfire on Windley Key, but found no one there injured. They proceeded south again along the road for another mile and a half. The group came across what they thought was a washout and spent the next two and a half hours trying to get across, even tying four men together with a downed electrical wire, but the water remained too swift and too deep. Only later did they learn that they had tried to cross Whale Harbor Channel. They finally gave up and walked back north to find outboards to circumvent the washout and continue their search for their fellow veterans.

◀ *The Bonus Army newspaper.*

▼ *Members of the Bonus Army marching across the Capitol Plaza in Washington, D.C., June 6, 1932, to demand Congressional approval of a bill that would have paid their long-promised war bonuses. (Underwood and Underwood/Corbis)*

▲ *The Florida State Road Department's dredge boat probably deepening the anchorage entrance at Camp 3 on Lower Matecumbe Key.*

▼ *Camp 3 under construction, March 1935.*

▲ *Camp 3 before the hurricane.*

◄ *Matecumbe Hotel, 1935. This was headquarters for the FERA administrators who oversaw the three work camps and the highway construction project.*

◄ *The houseboat* Sarasota, *anchored off Camp 3, housed the engineers from the Florida State Road Department who were supervising the highway construction. Colonel Sheeran moved the houseboat into Hurricane Creek, on the west side of Lower Matecumbe Key, before the storm arrived.*

July. 4 - 33

▲ *Vehicles waiting for the ferry at the landing next to Camp 3, July 1933. In the background is the Terminal Lunch.*

▲ *Ernest Hemingway's Key West house, 1938. (Bettmann/Corbis)*

▲ *Ernest Hemingway's study in his house in Key West. (Bob Krist/Corbis)*

▲ *Hemingway aboard his fishing boat,* Pilar.

▲ *Hemingway in Key West in the 1930s.*

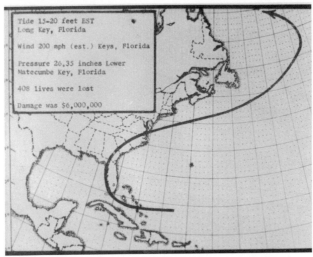

Tide 15-20 feet EST
Long Key, Florida

Wind 200 mph (est.) Keys, Florida

Pressure 26.35 inches Lower
Matecumbe Key, Florida

408 lives were lost

Damage was $6,000,000

◀ *The U.S. Weather Bureau's chart depicting the path of the storm from August 29– September 10, 1935.*

◀ *Relief worker holding one of the thirteen clocks found in the wreckage, all of them stopped at around 8:20 p.m..*

◄ *The Tavernier railroad depot (background) in the aftermath of the hurricane. The Overseas Highway runs through the middle of the photo.*

◄ *Camp 3 after the hurricane.*

◄ *The Lower Matecumbe Key ferry landing in the wake of the hurricane, looking north. Note the twisted rails to the right; they have been washed right off the railbed, which is to their right. The upper left portion of the photo shows the remains of the eastern portion of Camp 3, covered with sand. The ferry landing is in the center, and the wrecked ferryboat* Monroe County *is in the foreground.*

▲ *A close-up of the railbed near Camp 3, looking south. Note the rails, tossed in twisted disarray to the right of the bed.*

◄ *Remains of the Rustic Inn store and gasoline station, 1935. Owned by O. D. King, who also served as superintendent of the work camp vehicles, the store somehow survived the hurricane, though heavily damaged. It stood some four-tenths of a mile north of the Matecumbe Hotel.*

◄ *The lower floor of the ruined Matecume-be Hotel became a refuge for several survivors—including camp overseer Ray Sheldon—on the day after the storm.*

◄ Relief train in ruins near Islamorada, 1935. Only the locomotive remains on the tracks.

▼ Wreckage from the Islamorada post office/depot area is piled against the overturned relief train.

▲ *Snake Creek as seen from the Florida Bay side after the storm. Foot and vehicle traffic from the north (left) could proceed no farther until the bridges were repaired, so this became the staging area for relief efforts. A temporary wooden ramp and dock is seen on the bank-(foreground).*

▼ *Unloading a hurricane victim from a boat at Snake Creek.*

◀ *Floating bodies tethered to a piling near Islamorada.*

◀ *Bodies on the beach.*

▼ *Funeral pyre used for cremation ceremonies at Snake Creek. The crude boxes stacked in the back are caskets.*

◄ *Florida National Guardsmen and their gear.*

◄ *Relief workers at Snake Creek in line for chow or pay.*

▼ *The Florida Keys Memorial near the former site of the Matecumbe Hotel.*

CHAPTER TEN

Wednesday
September 4, 1935

As Tuesday night turned into Wednesday, helpers wandered in from Hollywood, Homestead, Miami, and other mainland towns that had been spared from the storm. Most were private citizens who had no connection to the camps other than concern for their fellow man. All the rescuers knew was what they could see when they made their way across Snake Creek in small boats.

Camp 1 had been obliterated. The hospital, formerly the Snake Creek Hotel, had been wiped off the Key. Nothing was left of it; even the foundation was washed away.

All the shocked, dazed, and injured survivors floating north across Snake Creek in small kicker boats in the early morning hours gave brief descriptions of the carnage. On his way across, John Good saw the body of George Sherman on what remained of Snake Creek Bridge. "[He] had a splinter driven through his forehead from the front between his eyes all the way through his head, protruding about four inches on both sides," Good said. Dr. Main's body lay nearby.

Only one newspaper reporter had ventured into the Upper Keys on Monday, William Johns of the *Miami Daily News,* and he had not been heard from since. The storm had severed the telephone and telegraph lines in the Keys, and further reports had been hindered by the destruction of the Snake Creek Bridge, but the *Miami Herald* noted that Homestead's hospitals were inundated with hurricane victims. "Widely conflicting reports as to the number of dead continued to come in to the *Herald* office until well after midnight," the paper's Wednesday edition said. Interviewing survivors, the newspaper published estimates of between 25 and 100 deaths below Snake Creek. The Red Cross predicted that fatalities wouldn't exceed 300.

Reports from the disaster area trickled in and made the papers. A pilot for Pan American, A. G. Parson, flew a Clipper to Havana in the morning and radioed to Miami:

Railroad and highway out, Upper Matecumbe to Lower Matecumbe. Bodies along course. Concrete bridges apparently okay. Railroad wrecked Long Key to Marathon. No visible life on Long Key; all buildings wrecked. Marathon not badly damaged.

Flying a Pan American Commodore to Miami from the Canal Zone, pilot William Doxy radioed:

Near railroad were eight coaches and three boxcars lying on their sides. Storm area appears as if broom had swept 40-mile swath through the Keys. Several small craft were blown on shore.

By morning 40 men from National Guard battalions in Miami and West Palm Beach had reached the Upper Keys and deployed to points south, mainly to prevent looting, trespassing, and to protect private property. They set up their command post in the partially completed Tavernier movie theater and put up a roadblock right outside. By Thursday their number would reach more than 180 troops. Like Guard units everywhere, they represented a cross section of American society, some wanting to serve their country, some needing the paycheck, some scrupulously honest, some not so honest. Based on survivors' reports, their behavior wasn't uniformly praiseworthy. "[All the National Guard had] done was to go down there and get drunk and get in the way and stop the ambulances from getting out," William Johns would later report.

Early Wednesday, William Kenneth Martin, Camp 5 timekeeper, reached Snake Creek from Miami, driving in a government car with Buck Wright, the purchasing agent for the bridge project. Since they were in a government car, the National Guard let them through. They boarded a kicker, rode it across Snake Creek, and landed in Camp 1. "We saw nothing standing," Martin said. "[T]imber was strewn everywhere—saw men pinned underneath and dead." The first man he recognized was Dr. Main. The pair walked to the Windley Key quarry and saw several bodies lying across or near the railroad tracks.

By 10:30 A.M., Martin and Wright had crossed Whale Harbor Channel in one of the small boats that had by then been pressed into service there and made it to Islamorada, where they found not one house standing along the beach. In the town itself only two shacks were standing, both belonging to O. D. King, but he and his family were nowhere to be found. All the other houses had blown into the Gulf. South of Islamorada they walked past the overturned train and counted seven bodies that the Pan Am pilot hadn't reported. One car had blown 400 feet, and all the water tanks were destroyed. Most of the nearby Matecumbe Hotel had blown away, but everyone inside what was left of it remained alive. Martin and Wright counted 98 dead altogether between Camp 1 and the southern end of Upper Matecumbe Key.

They didn't know it at the time, but O. D. King had already departed for the mainland. Mallie Pitman from Camp 1 had left the train wreckage earlier and walked to King's place. "About 10:00 A.M. [the rescuers] got us out," he said. "I came to Miami with Mr. King, his wife, and his wife's sister." Everyone in King's two shacks survived.

—⸰⸰⸰—

In the daylight calm, Ernest Hemingway weaved the *Pilar* slowly through the bodies floating and bobbing like garbage off what was left of the Camp 3 ferry slip. As the day grew hotter, with temperatures rising into the eighties, the bodies began baking, and the stench of death permeated the air.

Hemingway and his boat had come through the storm together unscathed in the Key West Navy Yard's submarine pen. The wind in Key West never exceeded 45 or 50 miles per hour, and by 5:00 A.M. on Tuesday, Hem's barometer started rising and the winds calmed a bit—the hurricane had passed them by. Having survived the long night aboard his boat, he walked back to his big house on Whitehead Street, which had suffered little, along with the rest of the city. Key West lost electrical power, and a few toppled trees and broken branches littered yards and streets, but there was no real damage. The city was cut off from the mainland, however— no telephone, no railroad.

Tuesday, the wind blew, the rains lashed down, and the sea remained turbulent, too much for a small boat to handle. But Tuesday night the skies cleared and the seas quieted. Hoping to explore the storm damage, Hemingway headed north on *Pilar* in the predawn darkness Wednesday morning with two Key West friends, Captain Eddie "Bra" Saunders and J. B. "Sully" Sullivan.

When *Pilar* approached Lower Matecumbe Key in the early afternoon after the 90-mile run from Key West, the landscape looked scoured except for two FERA water tanks that remained standing. All the construction equipment was blown over; sand had piled up two feet high on the center of the Key. "The island looked like the abandoned bed of a river where the sea had swept it," Hemingway wrote. All the brush had turned brown; the wind had stripped every green leaf from the branches. The mangroves held the majority of the dead suspended in their branches, twisted in grotesque, unnatural ways. A few of the bodies hung high, lifted there by the crest of the storm surge. "You found them everywhere and in the sun all of them were beginning to be too big for their blue jeans and jackets that they could never fill when they were on the bum and hungry," he said.

They set off up north to inspect Camp 5. He wrote his longtime editor at Scribner's, Max Perkins:

Max, you can't imagine it, two women, naked, tossed up into trees by the water, swollen and stinking, their breasts as big as balloons, flies between their legs. Then, by figuring, you locate where it is and recognize them as the two very nice girls who ran a sandwich place and filling-station three miles from the ferry. We located sixty-nine bodies where no one had been able to get in. Indian Key [less than a mile seaward between Up- per and Lower Matecumbe] absolutely swept clean, not a blade of grass, and over the high center of it were scat- tered live conchs that came in with the sea, craw fish,

and dead morays. The whole bottom of the sea blew
over it.

Hemingway also noticed an unusual absence of buzzards, which would normally have been picking at the flesh
of the dead. "Would you believe it?" he wrote. "The wind
killed all the buzzards and all the big winged birds like peli-
cans too." Blowflies, however, were all over the corpses. He
docked *Pilar* and the three men walked around, looking, in-
specting. Hem rolled one veteran over, a man who looked
about sixty. A land crab had chewed off his thumb. He found
one familiar face, Joe Lowe, a man on whom he had based
a character in his short story "One Trip Across." Lowe had
drowned. "You're dead now brother," Hemingway wrote in
an article published in the September 17 issue of *New Masses,*
"but who left you there in the hurricane months on the Keys
where a thousand men died before you when they were
building the road that's now washed out?"

He remembered drinking with Lowe and other veterans
at Key West, at Josie Grunt's place and Sloppy Joe's, and how
some of them "were punch drunk and some of them were
smart; some of them had been on the bum since the Argonne
almost and some had lost their jobs the year before last
Christmas; some had wives and some couldn't remember;
some were good guys, and others put their pay checks in
the Postal Savings and then came over to cadge in on the
drinks when better men were drunk; some liked to fight and

others liked to walk around the town; and they were all like what you get after a war." The more he thought about it, the more his outrage grew.

—⊗⊗⊗—

Reporter William Johns emerged from the overturned, strewn train car Wednesday morning and started heading north, following the tracks back out. He met up with Ray Sheldon, who was doing the same after his long night in the ruins of the Matecumbe Hotel, and the two men walked together. Sheldon seemed shaken, worried, and scared.

"Mr. Sheldon," Johns asked, "why in the devil weren't they taken out?"

"I don't know," Sheldon said. "I was in touch with Washington. I couldn't get the permission to take them off." He said Washington had told him to wait there until further developments. This was counter to what others would recall in later depositions, and Johns suspected as much based on his reporter's instinct and his Labor Day phone conversations with Sheldon. He wrote Sheldon's remarks off as a case of nerves. "Now, that man had gone through an awful lot," he said. "[M]aybe he was excited, and maybe it isn't the truth . . . I believed at the time when Sheldon told me that, that he was possibly mistaken." And there was one other bit of information he didn't put much credence in. "I have heard rumors, and rumors aren't any good, but I have heard rumors there was a squabble between the Florida East Coast Railway and the administration in Washington as to who was going to pay for it; and I know it is a lot of bunk," Johns said. A railroad, he knew, was a public utility, and was bound by law to help out during a disaster.

The reporter walked up to Whale Harbor, got ferried across, and then walked to Snake Creek, which he crossed Wednesday afternoon on a kicker. By then cars, trucks, and ambulances were lined up for two miles to help move out the survivors, and the CCC was constructing a hasty and flimsy footbridge across Snake Creek.

E. P. Rogers, who'd left Camp 1 on Friday and missed the hurricane, went to work in the Homestead hospital. "After I was there, I stayed from Wednesday morning until five o'clock then I told the ladies I was going down on the Keys and identify any of the men I possibly could," he said. Rogers managed to talk his way past the Guardsmen. "[By] the time I got there they were bringing the dead veterans from [Camp 1], they brought five or six men and I tried to identify them but you couldn't tell one from the other, their faces were all chewed and their eyes were out and I got nervous and had to leave."

Like Rogers, others just didn't have the stomach for identifying bodies. "Well, I looked at one and I quit," said Peter Fatten. "[They] were all so black, the first three I looked at were so black, I didn't look at no more, didn't make no more effort to look." And some simply weren't allowed to look by the authorities. "The only thing I can't understand is why they would not let us boys that were saved get over there and identify the others," said James R. Jones, who weathered the storm at Tavernier, six and a half miles north of Camp 1. "I believe a lot of those bodies could have been identified. . . . We just begged to get back and help identify the bodies." He and about thirty other camp survivors went all the way to Miami, met officials at the McAlister Hotel and pleaded to be allowed in, but the officials refused to hear them out.

———

That morning at 9:00 A.M., Mrs. Bradford and her pilot took off from Miami once again to search for her missing husband. The weather was clear, and they landed off the southern tip of Lower Matecumbe where Camp 3 and the store had once stood. Carson Bradford watched the seaplane land and emerged from the battered landscape to meet his wife. She ran up to him, hardly daring to believe he'd somehow survived. After everyone calmed down, someone noticed that the airplane had four seats—one more than needed—and Arthur Thilmann, who had hung by his feet Monday night from the tank car, was lying nearby with internal injuries. He didn't look like he'd last much longer without medical attention. With the help of a few of the vets, the pilot loaded Thilmann up into the spare seat and buckled him in. The Bradfords got in and the plane taxied across the water, picking up speed, skimming the tops of the waves, and lifting off north for Miami.

A short time later, around ten-thirty, another seaplane landed, this one from the Coast Guard, carrying two doctors. Between them they had only cotton balls and a bottle of rubbing alcohol.

When Blackie Pugh saw that, he lost his temper. "Why in hell didn't you bring a camera?" he yelled.

"Why?" one of the doctors asked.

"You didn't bring anything else," Pugh replied, "just sightseeing."

"We didn't know where we were going."

"You had a pretty good idea," Pugh shot back.

The airplane took off and flew back north for medical supplies.

Those two airplanes were the first communication Camp 3 had with the outside world. No one else landed on Lower Matecumbe until after noon, when Hemingway's visit was followed by the arrival of a twin-engine amphibian loaned to the Red Cross and carrying doctors. The pilot, Roy Keeler, radioed back to Miami:

> About 20 miles of railroad track torn off right of way. Landed at Tavernier at 11:45 and secured medical supplies, which we flew to Lower Matecumbe, being the first relief to reach there. Conditions most serious from Tavernier to Matecumbe, with many dead laid out and a great many people walking around without shelter, waiting for relief. . . . Survivors of Camp 5, numbering

11, are at Camp 3, all others perished. At Camp 3 are
45 known dead, 25 wounded, and 75 refugees. Coast
Guard cutter just arrived at 2:15 P.M.

The Coast Guard cutter was accompanied by two smaller
boats and followed by a yacht, the *Byronic*. The *Byronic*
belonged to the Millers, a wealthy couple who split their time
between Miami and New York. They were in Manhattan, but
their crew had piloted the yacht down carrying two doctors
and medical supplies. "Then of course those that was hurt
the worst, they put them on this private yacht, took them to
Miami to the hospital," Frank Ballas said. There were De Forrest Rumage, who'd fractured his back, and Jacob Nonnenman, with a cold and a sore chest. The balance, some 130 survivors, including Blackie Pugh, left soon after on the Red
Cross plane and the Coast Guard cutter.

Twelve men volunteered to stay behind with Camp 3 superintendent Ben Davis and help with the dead. When they
identified a body, Davis scratched the name on a piece of
wood. Many were simply unrecognizable. One by one the
veterans carried their comrades to the dock and laid them out
on planks, wrapped in sheets.

But at 4:00 P.M. the National Guard contingent from Key
West marched in and announced to Davis that they were
now in charge and that Davis and his men should leave.
"Captain Davis had quite a controversy with them about it
as he did not want to leave," Arthur Brown recalled. Brown

was sure he could still identify more of the dead—he was camp timekeeper, after all. "I knew pretty near every man in the reservation," he said, "and Mr. Davis did also."

The vets told the Guardsmen where more bodies could be found, but the Guardsmen didn't seem to make much of a move in that direction. Like many locals, the Guard didn't accord much respect to the veterans, dead or alive. "There seemed to be some laxity on the part of the National Guard when they took hold," Brown said. "Of course it took a lot of work as the mangroves had to be cut before the bodies could be gotten out of the water, and it was a big job. However, they were very lax in taking part in the work." The vets continued at it for a few hours, until dark, "and we were all worn out and tired by that time," said Griffin, "and the bodies began to decompose; you could touch them and flesh would fall off." Still, feeling as if they were back in combat, the old soldiers were determined that no man would be left behind.

When the last twelve veterans pulled out of Camp 3 for Snake Creek, the Guardsmen cautioned them about talking publicly about the hurricane. "I told one National Guardsman that if anyone wanted a statement from me no one would stop me from telling my story," Brown said.

Far to the north, the hurricane passed offshore of Tampa, where seawater flooding the streets mixed with five inches of rain that had fallen over the previous twenty-four hours. Tampa's seawall collapsed before the storm moved on.

⊗≋⊗

The owner of the Matecumbe Hotel, Captain Ed Butters, set out on foot for Miami with his family Wednesday afternoon, having heard that boats were ferrying survivors across Whale Harbor Channel and Snake Creek. Butters had a puncture wound in his foot, and his wife, Fern, had a sprained ankle. Their faces and eyes were red and raw. They limped past dead bodies, some of whom they recognized. Finally reaching the Snake Creek embankment, they saw corpses stacked under a canvas shroud, some with children's feet poking out. Finally Fern could take no more, and she fainted. When she came to they were in a boat crossing the channel.

Butters had left Jim Burnett, a trusted employee, in charge of what was left of the hotel. When the National Guard arrived that afternoon, a pair of officers saw Butters's new Plymouth sedan—just five months old—sitting outside and asked Burnett whose car it was.

"Captain Butters, who just left for Miami," he replied.

They asked for the key.

Burnett said he didn't have it—and Butters didn't want it started.

"We don't need Butters' permission, or anyone else's," one of the officers told Burnett. "The island is under martial law," he said. If they could get the car started, they were going to use it.

They broke the right front window and opened the door, then one got in and stepped on the starter, which kicked salt water up into the pistons. They drained the battery trying to start it, then pried open the trunk to get tools. There were two suitcases in the trunk, and they opened one of them and tossed the contents on the ground.

One officer said that they didn't need the car anyway—and even if they could get it started, where would they drive to? But they warned Burnett not to leave the property or go on to anyone else's, that they were staying right there on the Key that night and if they wanted that car they were coming back to get it. Then one of them picked up the intact suitcase, and they both walked away.

That wasn't the only such incident. Eugene Lowkis, of Camp 1, and another vet came across the body of a veteran whom they could identify by the Masonic ring on his finger. He was a big man, and he lay a distance from the Camp 3 ferry slip, so they went to get some help moving the body over there. When they returned with help, they found the body surrounded by National Guardsmen, and he had been turned over, his pockets pulled inside out, and the ring taken from his finger. Lowkis went to the officer in charge and asked him to search the men for the missing ring.

"They've already been searched," the officer replied.

—◦◦◦◦—

The first doctor to reach Camp 5, Dr. G. C. Franklin, came down from Coconut Grove. The veterans who met him led Dr. Franklin to Elmer Kressberg, lying there impaled by the two-by-four. Dr. Franklin looked Kressberg over and told him it would have to be removed. He offered him a shot of morphine, but Kressberg refused, asking instead for two beers. Someone scrounged them up and gave them to him. Kressberg drank both, one after the other, and looked up at the doctor. "Now pull," he said. Dr. Franklin grabbed the timber firmly and jerked it out. Kressberg died a few minutes later.

At Snake Creek, which became the local center of disaster relief, Dr. J. A. Smith, a country doctor, performed triage on the survivors, then sent the worst cases on to the Post Graduate Hospital in Homestead until it was full. Then Homestead officials opened up the schoolhouse as a hospital and shelter, and someone made their own house available for shelter, and the Baptists donated their Sunday school. And all day long, James L. King used the ambulance he'd escaped Camp 1 in to carry wounded from the field hospital on Snake Creek to hospitals in Miami.

The uninjured needed food, clothes, and blankets as well as shelter. Civil engineer Hubert Campbell Nichols of Homestead said, "My wife was here and she made up ten or twelve gallons of coffee and that much soup or more and I would come in and get some of each and take it over [to the schoolhouse] and gave it to them as they came in, and gave a blanket and pillow and they put them on the floor. That is all we could do and they went to sleep."

Members of the Homestead fire department continued working far into the night, still helping the injured, still rescuing men pinned beneath shacks, vehicles, and debris, taking them to Snake Creek as they had been doing since Tuesday. Then the National Guard ran them out.

CHAPTER ELEVEN

Wednesday Evening
September 4, 1935
and After

I n *To Have and Have Not*, the only novel Hemingway set
in Key West, he portrayed an America divided into two
classes. On Monday, September 2, while hundreds of indigent veterans—the have-nots—fought for their lives on the
Upper Keys, an entirely different class of people—the
haves—endured the hurricane in a 426-foot, 8,000-ton
steamship called the *Dixie*.

The flagship of the Morgan Line, "elegant" barely sufficed
to describe the *Dixie*. The all-steel vessel, completed in May
1927, had cost $2.5 million ($335.5 million in 2003 dollars).
Every safety measure had been incorporated into its

construction. She had twelve metal lifeboats, enough for all passengers, in accordance with regulations enacted after the *Titanic* disaster of 1912. Each lifeboat was equipped with a rapid lowering device, and the ship had a radio direction finder to help the navigator plot accurate bearings. The interior decor was Colonial; the public rooms included a library, smoking room, lounge, café, barbershop, observation room, and even a sun parlor. Each stateroom had its own telephone and hot and cold running water, and most had a private bathroom. The crew of 123 catered to every whim of *Dixie*'s 233 passengers, who had signed up for a cruise from New Orleans to New York. Among them were several honeymooners, three popularity contest winners from Pennsylvania, and an NBC radio engineer.

The trip had started out a bit dull to some. "It's too monotonous and I'll be glad to get off," wrote a bored Charlotte Evans of Philadelphia to her mother. "It's the quietest crowd I ever saw, and there's no excitement." Then, sailing north and east of the Keys, the *Dixie* met up with the thrill of a lifetime.

At 8:12 P.M. on Monday, the hurricane tossed the steamship aground on French Reef, within sight of Key Largo—had it been possible to see Key Largo during the storm. Four minutes after her bottom scraped the reef, radio officer James W. Hodges sent out his first SOS. But the antenna had broken in the fierce wind, and although several ships received the signal, it was too weak to trace. So, risking his life, Henry Tregor, the NBC engineer, climbed the stack and rigged another antenna. "I never expected to get down safely," Tregor said. "The wind fairly burned me."

This time other ships received the message loud and clear, but they were busy fighting their own battles. By 8:45 P.M.—nearly the same time the relief train was blown off the tracks and Frenchy Fecteau's watch stopped—the 233 passengers panicked and tried to abandon ship. But the deck hands calmly placed life belts on them and herded them to their boat stations along the lee rail while stewards passed among them handing out coffee and sandwiches. After an hour, Captain Einer William Sundstrom believed the seas were still too dangerous and refused to give the order to abandon ship. To calm themselves while the *Dixie* rocked, her passengers began singing "The Man on the Flying Trapeze." Eventually they started believing that the ship might hold together, and they filed into the public rooms for more singing and more drinking.

While the *Dixie* rolled and creaked, sewage and seawater flooded the staterooms and finally the public rooms. But the fifty-year-old Captain Sundstrom, who had first gone to sea at age sixteen, remained calm and kept her pumps working. The passengers kept on singing and drinking, and forty-six hours later the seas finally calmed enough to evacuate everyone to the United Fruit liner *Limon* and the steamship *Reaper*. Despite having sprained both ankles, Sundstrom personally tied the safety line around each passenger's waist. A few days later, after things quieted down, tugs pulled the *Dixie* off the reef and towed her north to the

Jersey shipyard where she had been built. All 356 on board made it off safely.

Back on the Keys, the final Red Cross estimates of the dead reached 405, of which 250 were veterans.

———∞∞∞———

The hurricane still had work ahead of it. By Wednesday afternoon it was flooding the Florida Gulf Coast north of Tampa and causing extensive damage to coastal structures and fishing boats. Three additional lives were lost along the coast before the storm made its second landfall in rural Taylor County, east of Tallahassee. There it destroyed or heavily damaged more than 500 homes. In CCC Company 1410, which had just been set up in Foley, the only casualty was the camp kitchen. By late Wednesday night the storm was spinning through Georgia, heading toward the Carolinas.

———∞∞∞———

Ray Sheldon finally arrived in Miami Wednesday evening, an exhausted and burdened man, and there he met another such man, Fred Ghent, who was waiting with a court stenographer to record Sheldon's statement about the events of the past few days. The full extent of the tragedy was no longer deniable, even for Ghent. Its crushing weight must have borne down on both men's shoulders. There would be, in all probability, sleepless nights of self-recrimination ahead, but now was a time to defend, from the world at large and from private demons.

The essence of Sheldon's statement was that he'd tracked the hurricane closely since Saturday and that the Weather Bureau had simply missed the turn north and thus failed to provide adequate warning. It was an explanation that absolved Ghent as well as Sheldon, and no doubt Ghent was pleased with it. It is entirely possible that Sheldon believed it sincerely. He had, indeed, tracked the storm's progress with thumbtacks across a map, making an engineer's calculations of probability and cost-benefit. His failure was one of imagination. He had imagined those thumbtacks as representing the extent of the storm, not its center, not seeing that even if those thumbtacks marched through the Straits of Florida as forecast, the camps were not safe. And he had projected the storm's past track, which was known with reasonable confidence, into a future that he imagined could be described with equal confidence. He had played dice with a hurricane, gambling the safety of 400 men.

—⁂—

Early Thursday morning a Coast Guard cutter departed the Camp 3 landing on Lower Matecumbe Key bearing the bodies of 38 veterans and steamed to the Snake Creek disaster relief staging area some 13 miles away. But once it got there, no one on the boat or ashore was eager to unload the ghastly cargo. "The stench was something that made men turn and leave the vicinity," said one Red Cross rescue worker. Finally the Coast Guard crew started dropping the bodies into the water so that men from shore could wade in and pull them to land. When a Red Cross worker reached the first corpse, the man's scalp came off in his hand.

The *Dixie*'s plight received big play in the papers, almost as much as the veterans' camps. Huge headlines splashed across the front pages of the *Miami Herald* and the *New York Times*—especially the *Times*, since most of the passengers were from Manhattan. In *Time* magazine's coverage of the storm, the first two and a half columns of the five-column story focused on the *Dixie*.

Then other news shoved the storm from the headlines. A few days after the storm, an assassin's bullet cut down former Governor and current Senator Huey Long of Louisiana, a radical populist who had just announced that he would run for president in 1936. Then Italy invaded Ethiopia, and Mussolini announced that he expected war with England. Germany passed laws revoking citizenship for Jews, including the Fatherland's own World War I veterans. The Detroit Tigers beat the Chicago Cubs four games to two in the World Series. And Howard Hughes set the new land speed record of 352 miles per hour in his new Hughes Racer. Time marched on.

On Friday, September 6, the dozen men whom the National Guard had forced from their work in Camp 3 on Wednesday arrived at Camp Foster, near Jacksonville, joining 200 others already sent there by train. "We had not been there over three days when they advised that they would send us down to the office of the CCC's, and tried to ship us out without giving us a chance to be reimbursed in any manner whatsoever for our personal losses, etc.," said Arthur Brown. The men telegrammed Ben Davis to come up and represent them, and three days later he arrived. The men got their money.

That same day, Florida Governor David Sholtz flew over the Upper Keys in a Coast Guard airplane to inspect the devastation firsthand. Approaching the Matecumbes, Sholtz grew more and more horrified by the sights below. The Keys turned from lush to scoured bare, the railroad tracks from shiny and parallel to mangled, then washed away completely. He saw wrecked houses and camps; blackened corpses dotted the landscape. When he landed, Sholtz declared himself "shocked beyond words" by what he had seen. Then he ordered the victims' bloated bodies to be cremated, as public health officials had been recommending, rather than flown out for burial.

Veterans groups and Floridians alike protested. There was, after all, no fresh water to infect, and many of the dead had yet to be identified. While they couldn't exactly be buried there on the Keys—solid limestone lay just below the surface—there was still time for proper burial elsewhere. FDR had announced from Hyde Park the day before that veterans killed by the storm would be flown home or buried at Arlington National Cemetery, according to their families' wishes, but it was now clear that the decomposition of the bodies and the impossibility of identifying many of the victims made that plan unfeasible. Working nonstop Friday and Saturday, Roosevelt Administration officials organized a Sunday burial and memorial service for many of the victims at Miami's Woodlawn Cemetery.

Even Miami, however, was beyond reach for the decomposing bodies at the Snake Creek staging area. There the stench grew worse with each passing hour, and corpses fell apart during handling. In accordance with public health officials' recommendations and the governor's orders, National Guardsmen set about building a funeral pyre of thirty-six pine coffins. Those few veterans who hadn't been hospitalized or interred at Camp Foster on the mainland were now enlisted to handle the dead. Two such men—Leonard LeCatta, a member of the veterans' camps for just one month, and H. P. Williams—came across one battered corpse whom they searched before carrying it off for cremation. In his pocket they found his wallet: It was Glenn Robinson, superintendent of Camp 5. They also found $54 in cash and a check for $25 made out to W. K. Martin, the camp timekeeper. The two turned over the check and cash to a doctor, who in turn handed them over to Major William Albury, commander of Key West's Florida National Guard unit. Then LeCatta and Williams carried Robinson's body to the pyre, where flames consumed it with the others.

For three days and nights following the storm, Frederick Poock of Camp 5, the man in charge of the camp trust deposits, worked without sleep in Homestead helping with the evacuation. Friday was his first chance to get back to the Matecumbe Hotel, but when he arrived it was after dark, and what was left of the place was locked up. He returned the next day in a speedboat, got into the hotel, and retrieved his records. "They were water-logged but practically intact," he said. Everyone who'd made deposits would get paid back in full.

Only one man tried to chisel cash from the fund: Wadie Essau of Camp 1. At Homestead he came forward and maintained that he'd deposited $55. "At that time it was not generally known that my records had been saved," Poock said. But eventually Essau experienced a fit of remorse or honesty. Removed shortly afterward to Camp Foster, he was asked by an investigator whether he had anything in the fund, and this time Essau replied that he did not. Case closed. Willard Parker, meanwhile, pressed his claim of losing $5,000 during the storm when forced to use his belt to strap himself to wreckage. No one believed him. The average annual salary in 1935, after all, was $1,500, and Parker had been earning $30 a month.

On Friday morning, September 6, the storm blew out into the Atlantic again at the mouth of the Chesapeake Bay after knocking down utility poles in the Carolinas and flooding coastal Maryland and Delaware. Over the ocean it intensified once more, and ships along its northward track reported hurricane-force winds and pressures as low as 28.02 inches between Friday and Sunday evenings. By Monday evening, a week after descending on the Matecumbes, the storm was rapidly weakening in the cold waters southeast of Greenland, and the following day its remnants merged with a high-latitude low. Its real mission—to disperse heat from the tropics to higher latitudes—was complete.

The wind had barely stopped blowing before the inquiries began. On Friday, September 6, three separate investigations were launched: one by Harry Hopkins, chief administrator of the Works Progress Administration and FERA, who sent assistant WPA director Aubrey Williams to Florida; one by Florida State Attorney George Ambrose Worley; and a third by the American Legion on behalf of its fellow veterans. All three focused on two things: the Weather Bureau's reports and the delayed relief train.

Right away, though, it seemed as if the first two investigations had reached their conclusions before they'd begun. "I think it is a terrible and a shocking disaster," Hopkins told a reporter. "But I don't think from the weather reports—which I've been reading—that anybody would necessarily have evacuated those people." It was the message Ghent had conveyed to FERA officials in Washington after taking Sheldon's statement. Arriving in Florida Friday morning, Aubrey Williams made one flight over the Upper Keys and interviewed a dozen witnesses while Sheldon sat in the room observing—hardly a formula for frank or negative testimony. Williams then read six witness transcripts from the state investigation and had his report on Hopkins and Roosevelt's desks by Sunday afternoon. "It is impossible for us to reach the conclusion that there has been negligence or mistaken judgment on the part of those charged with the responsibility for the safety of the men engaged on the Keys projects," the report read. "To our mind, the catastrophe must be characterized as an 'act of God.' " Julius Stone, director of the Florida Emergency Relief Administration and self-proclaimed mastermind of the Keys work camps, had suggested the act of God conclusion on Thursday.

And as *Time* magazine reported, "After a four-day investigation, during which he queried Weather Bureau officials, camp officials and residents of the storm-wrecked Florida Keys, State Attorney George Ambrose Worley last week came to the conclusion that no one was responsible for the failure to evacuate veterans. . . . 'There will be no indictments or recommendations of indictments,' said he, bundling up his report and speeding it off by automobile to Governor Dave Sholtz at Jacksonville."

But veterans' groups found the hasty investigations lacking. In its own investigation, the American Legion even heard a stunning additional allegation: A. J. Wheeler, adjutant of the American Legion's Harvey Seeds Post in Miami, testified before a legion committee that "the officers deserted when the storm approached and left the men to their fate," adding that at least one veteran maintained the relief train had been made up the day before the storm but couldn't leave Miami until it received permission from Washington. Other veterans' organizations bared their fangs. John Skillman, who commanded Miami's chapter of the Veterans of Foreign Wars, said Williams had "whitewashed" the whole affair. According to the *Tampa Tribune*, Skillman alleged that "veterans' committees thrice sought from Ray Sheldon . . . permission to leave before the storm struck only to be threatened with guards to keep them there," and said he had sixty-seven veterans' affidavits demanding President Roosevelt investigate.

At the sweltering annual VFW convention in New Orleans just a few days later, the organization's national commander, James E. Van Zandt, told the crowd that the doomed veterans had been sent down to the Keys to prevent yet another Bonus March on Washington. Later, in Washington, Van Zandt mirrored Skillman's assessment of the investigation as a whitewash and asked for President Roosevelt to "punish officials responsible."

While piloting *Pilar* back to Key West, Hemingway, too, grew determined to say something about the tragedy. Back in his expansive, hurricane-proof home, he sat down in his study and scribbled out a searing essay titled "Who Murdered the Vets?" *New Masses*, the official voice of the American Communist Party, published it in the September 17 issue. He wrote:

> They're better off, I can hear whoever sent them say, explaining it to himself. What good were they? You can't account for accidents or acts of God. They were well-fed, well-housed, well-treated and let us suppose, now they are well dead.
>
> But I would like to make whoever sent them there carry just one out through the mangroves, or turn one

over that lay in the sun along the fill, or tie five together so they won't float out, or smell that smell you thought you'd never smell again, with luck when rich bastards make a war. The lack of luck goes on until all who take part in it are gone. . . .

You're dead now brother, but who left you there in the hurricane months on the Keys where a thousand men died before you when they were building the road that's washed out now?

Who left you there? And what's the punishment for manslaughter now?

Just a few weeks after the storm, the Federal Steamship Inspection Board absolved Captain Einer Sundstrom from any blame for the grounding of the *Dixie* on French Reef. The weather, the board determined, deserved the entire blame.

While the ink was drying on the preliminary investigations into the veterans' deaths, the memorial service in Miami also proceeded. In Woodlawn Cemetery, just after 10:00 A.M. on the sunny Sunday morning of September 8, crowds of people, a few in uniform, swarmed through the iron gates. They gathered around eighty-two metal-lined coffins with hastily embalmed bodies set one foot apart in four long trenches dug the night before—trenches nearly as deep as the ones the men in the coffins had huddled in during the Great War. Three wreaths sat among scattered poppies, symbolic of the war dead from a poem written in 1915 by Canadian army physician John McCrae: "In Flanders field the poppies grow / Between the crosses, row on row." A National Guardsman—who only a few days earlier guarded the Keys against looters and veterans who wanted to help identify the dead—stood at the head of each casket, many containing unidentified bodies, and Navy Admiral E. B. Fenner and Army General George Van Horn also stood, bowing their heads. Colonel George E. Ijams, assistant director of the Veterans Administration, representing FDR, presented the eulogy. A priest, a rabbi, and a minister performed the rites. As the reverend finished his prayer the last flag-draped coffin—the only one not laid in the trench prior to the ceremony—slowly descended. National Guardsmen then retrieved the flags from the caskets and quickly but carefully folded them into triangles. They stepped back, and a bugler stepped forward. Seven National Guardsmen simultaneously fired three times, and slowly, mournfully, the bugler blew "Taps."

That evening Miami held a second ceremony, this time to honor all the dead, veteran and civilian alike. Some 15,000 crowded into the Bayfront Amphitheater—spilling over into the aisles, back, and sides—and Colonel Ijams read another statement from the president expressing his "profound grief and deep sense of loss because of the tragic death of the defenders of the nation." When the colonel was finished, a band played "Nearer My God to Thee," while the mourners bowed their heads. The entire ceremony lasted forty-five minutes.

More than a month later, corpses were still turning up. The body of George Pepper, who'd left in Ben Davis's car during the hurricane, washed up near Cape Sable, on the southwestern tip of the Florida mainland, approximately 40 miles from the Matecumbes. Davis's 1934 Dodge lay submerged 100 feet offshore between Upper and Lower Matecumbe.

—⊷⊶⊷—

Despite Colonel Ijams's yeoman's duty in Florida on behalf of the Roosevelt Administration, the Veterans Administration wasn't satisfied with the hasty investigations of the federal and Florida governments. On September 11, Ijams's boss, VA director General Frank Hines, assigned David Kennamer, a staunch Republican born in Alabama, to conduct a thorough investigation. Kennamer formed teams that tracked down every survivor and recorded their depositions. The investigators asked the same questions over and over: What is your name, age, and residence? Do you have any relatives? Are you a veteran? Have you been employed at one of the veterans' camps on the Keys? Were you employed there at the time of the hurricane on September 2nd? Were you in the camp during the hurricane? Were you injured? Where? Did anyone discourage you from leaving camp before the storm? Did anyone attempt to leave by truck? Has anyone attempted to prevent you from making any statement? And the clincher: Who do you think is responsible?

One Camp 3 veteran took this opportunity, perhaps the only time anyone had asked his opinion on anything, to answer that last question as formally as he knew how:

I, Jacob Sacks, want to go down on the record that there is nobody else responsible for that cold blooded murder but Ghent of this Jacksonville office, he is the sole man responsible for the loss of lives and that sure it was an act of God, Aubrey Williams gave out in a statement to the press that it was an act of God, yes I agree with him on that as far as the property and the hurricane are concerned but the loss of lives I accuse Mr. Ghent and nobody else is responsible because he wanted to get a feather in his hat with the officials of the FERA by having the price of the train and he endangered the lives of about one thousand men with three or four hundred dollars.

Another, Charles McClary, also from Camp 3, spooned on the praise for Ben Davis: "As for Mr. Davis, he was a man amongst men; he done the best he could, no blame laid on his soul whatsoever."

Most blamed Ghent and Sheldon, though someone occasionally blamed an odd one, such as Sheeran. One man even blamed Blackie Pugh. Some of the testimony was simply poignant:

Q: Did anyone make any effort during Sunday and Monday to keep you from leaving the camp if you wanted to?
Justus Schadt (Camp 3): No, but we all depended upon our leaders, in other words, we thought we were working for the government, and the government ain't going to let us be

blown to pieces; I thought the government is going to take care of me. If I was working for a little contractor—but I was working for the United States government, and I thought they would take care of us.

Some of it pointed to a cover-up:

Q: Did you hear him [Sheldon] or anyone else admonish anyone not to tell what they knew about the storm?
D. A. Malcolm (auditor, FERA): Not in the box car [where Sheldon weathered the storm until the relief train arrived].
Q: Anyplace else?
Malcolm: Yes. In Miami I heard Mr. Cutler make the remark that we should protect the Administration.

At least one questioner went so far as to record his impressions of the subject. At the bottom of Raleigh LePreux's deposition, one prim hand wrote, "Mr. LePreux had been drinking."

The grilling of the camp leaders, though—Sheldon, Ghent, Van Hyning, Sheldon's secretary, Mrs. L. A. Fritchman, Blackie Pugh, William Hardaker, Sam Cutler, Ben Davis, Albert Buck—Kennamer left for himself.

Kennamer: Do you feel there was some carelessness and negligence in connection with this matter?
Buck: Yes, sir.
Kennamer: In what way?

Buck: Well, because they waited too long. In other words, on Sunday Mr. Sheldon was in Key West honeymooning; Mr. Ghent was in Jacksonville or some other place; and we was getting reports all over the country—in other words, from all over the country—that this storm was approaching, and Mr. Cutler was there in charge without any authority.

At times the tone turned confrontational, the testimony defensive:

Kennamer: Was Mr. Cutler very much alarmed?
Fritchman: Yes.
Kennamer: How about the others around headquarters?
Fritchman: Well, there was no one there to be concerned, I don't think.
Kennamer: What did the others think of the situation? Were they in accord with Mr. Cutler's?
Fritchman: No, they thought he was unduly alarmed.
Kennamer: Who were the people who thought he was unduly alarmed?
Fritchman: I can't remember who was there Sunday. I mentioned Mr. Patterson [sic], Mr. Good and Mr. Malcolm who I know was there. I didn't see any of them criticize him.
Kennamer: Were they in accord with what he was doing, or what he thought about the situation?
Fritchman: I will tell you who was in accord with Mr. Cutler, and that was Jones. I remember he said that Cutler was right.
Kennamer: What did you think about it?

Fritchman: I thought he was unnecessarily alarmed because the warnings were not alarming. I had been in so many of them I was not excited at all.

Kennamer: You did think that a storm was immediate in that section didn't you?

Fritchman: Its intensity had not been mentioned, and it always had been in previous years.

Kennamer: Does hurricane force indicate intensity?

Fritchman: It always says of greater or lesser intensity. They always told us the intensity of the storm.

Kennamer: Hurricane force indicates severe intensity, doesn't it?

Or this interrogation of Sheldon's friend, William Hardaker:

Q: I will ask you to examine what purports to be advisories sent out by Weather Bureau at 2:56 A.M., and 10 A.M., September 1st, 1935, and 3:30 A.M., September 2nd, 1935, and state if these warnings (handing same to witness) indicate that the camps were in danger?

Hardaker: Am I being the judge of the Weather Bureau now?

Q: Well, would that put you on notice that these areas might be in danger?

Hardaker: Well (reading weather advisories)—will you please state your question now?

Q: I asked, if you received those advisories, would that have put you on notice that this area might have been in danger?

Hardaker: Yes, I believe I would.

Q: If you had seen that advisory sent out at 3:30 that morning, you would have been somewhat alarmed yourself, wouldn't you?

Hardaker: Yes, I think so.

Q: Would you have taken any definite action or insisted upon Mr. Sheldon taking definite action to get the men out of there?

Hardaker: No, I would not have insisted on Mr. Sheldon, because he was the man at the gun there, and I would not have thought it was my business to tell him what to do.

The report ran to 400 pages by the time Kennamer handed it over to General Hines on October 30. In it, Kennamer placed the blame on Sheldon, Ghent, and Van Hyning. Despite the questionable accuracy of the Weather Bureau's reports, Kennamer wrote, they were good enough to alert the three to impending danger. Sheldon, the report said, shouldn't have countermanded Cutler's orders to close the canteens, and he should have had Ghent order the train earlier. His 5:00 A.M. call from Key West on Sunday should have been warning enough for Ghent to order the train there and then. Ghent should have remained in contact with the camps and Sheldon; he should never have disappeared as he did Sunday and Monday while the hurricane bore down on the Matecumbes. Van Hyning should have had a firm agreement with the railroad to provide emergency trains in the first place. He should have been in contact with Ghent. About the only blameless party was the railroad—which no one warned in time to send a train (or trains) down to the camps—and especially the relief train's crew, which did in fact start south from Miami within two and a half hours of finally receiving the request from Ghent, risking their lives in a vain attempt to rescue the veterans.

But Kennamer's investigation had no impact. General Hines gave a copy of the report to Aubrey Williams with the understanding that Williams would pass it along to FDR, but Williams never did. Roosevelt never saw it.

But that wasn't the end of the matter. In January 1936, Congress voted to award World War I veterans their bonus. Roosevelt vetoed the bill, and Congress quickly overrode his veto. The vets began receiving their money in June.

That March a committee consisting of fourteen Democrats, six Republicans, and one Progressive Party member was formed in the House of Representatives to investigate the hurricane tragedy under the auspices of HR 9486, "A bill for the relief of widows, children and dependent parents of World War veterans who died as a result of the Florida hurricane at Windley Island and Matecumbe Keys September 2, 1935."

The committee was headed by Democrat John Elliot Rankin of Mississippi. Born in 1882 and a congressman since 1921, Rankin supported separation of the races and would go on to call for the internment of Japanese-American civilians after the Pearl Harbor attack, categorize World War II as an "international Jewish plot," and say that the real enemy in that war wasn't Nazi Germany but the Soviet

Union. He later threw his support behind the House Un-American Activities Committee. But he was a Dixie Democrat—with the emphasis on "Democrat," an ardent supporter of FDR—and as such his mission was to protect the policies of his party.

The thorn in his side during the hearings proved to be Edith Nourse Rogers, a Republican from Massachusetts. Representative Rogers had been elected to fill the seat of her late husband, John Jacob Rogers, who died in 1925. During his time in the House, she had volunteered and worked for the YMCA, the Red Cross, and veterans' hospitals; in Congress she had sponsored legislation to form the Women's Army Corps and would become one of the authors of the GI Bill of Rights.

Rankin despised her.

The hearings began Thursday, March 26, 1936, and concluded on Saturday, May 9. During those six weeks, the committee called twenty-three witnesses, ranging from the head of the FERA to Mrs. Laura Van Ness, the wife of Benjamin Van Ness, who had been swept away by the tidal wave. Aubrey Williams, author of the two-day investigation for FDR's right-hand man Harry Hopkins, also testified, as did Ghent, Sheldon, and Van Hyning. Rankin lobbed softballs; Edith Rogers asked the tough questions. Sheldon's testimony showed the dynamic at work:

Rogers: Did you have enough trucks to take them away in?
Sheldon: There were trucks down there; yes.

Rogers: Did you have enough?

Sheldon: I believe there were trucks enough to take them away; yes.

Rogers: It would have been cheaper to have sent them out by truck, would it not?

Sheldon: It was not a question of money, it was a question of doing what should have been done.

Rogers: But it would have been quicker, much quicker, to get them out that way, rather than have waited for the train?

Sheldon: We had no reason to have the train. We had no storm, from outward appearances, that was going to hit the Keys, at that time.

Rogers: But they do—storms sometimes change their courses?

Sheldon: That is what the record shows.

Rogers: They often do that?

Sheldon: Yes.

Rogers: And in your experience, they have changed their course, often?

Sheldon: Of storms, there is no telling where they will go.

Rogers: So you have to be ready to move at once?

Then Rankin abruptly steered the questioning in another direction:

Rankin: Mr. Sheldon, right there, what was the attitude of the people who lived on the Keys; were they excited over the storm?

Sheldon: Some of them closed and got the boards together to nail up their houses, and some of them did nail them, but that was done, because if there was a storm, it was a whole lot easier to nail them up during pleasant weather than to wait until the last minute and get out in the rain and struggle with the boards.

As for the question of having the relief train ready, Chairman Rankin noted during Sheldon's testimony that "a railroad is a public utility and they are under as much obligation to have their trains ready in case of these disasters, as if they were dealing with the government, itself, or with a state." His statement implied that Sheldon, Ghent, or Van Hyning could not be blamed for not ordering the train. It was probably the railroad's fault. Not one of the witnesses represented the railroad—Rankin had made sure of that. The committee hadn't paid a Florida East Coast Railway official's way up to testify.

And so the hearing went. When Rogers asked the witnesses probing questions, Rankin would interrupt her, soften the interrogation, and even attack Rogers, sometimes all in one sentence. Rankin's committee found little fault in the actions of the Federal Emergency Relief Administration, Sheldon, Ghent, Van Hyning, the Weather Bureau, or any government agency for that matter. In short, the six-week congressional hearing only confirmed to the American people the validity of the hasty investigations of Aubrey Williams and George Worley. No one was to blame. The tragedy had been an act of God. On June 1 the House passed its bill, awarding $217 per month to the family of every veteran who had died in the hurricane.

Nearly a year and a half later FDR easily won his second term. By that time the Labor Day Hurricane was long forgotten, but not the plight of American veterans. Sixteen days after the invasion of Normandy, on June 22, 1944, Roosevelt—after initially favoring more modest legislation—signed into law the GI Bill of Rights that had been championed by the American Legion and newspaper baron William Randolph Hearst. Veterans of the Second World War would receive federal aid to pay for businesses, homes, education, and hospitalization. The education benefits alone would cost the federal government $14.5 billion, but the return on investment would be immeasurable. According to a 1986 study, each dollar invested under the bill yielded between $5 and $12 in tax revenues. Perhaps more to the point, the GI Bill would be perhaps the foremost factor in the postwar growth of the American middle class—a Marshall Plan for America, as historians have said, a transformative force.

Following the 1935 Labor Day Hurricane the United States Weather Bureau defended itself from critics, most of whom were fellow government officials anxious to shift blame. In an article written in October for the "Monthly Weather Review," a Weather Bureau publication, Washington employee

W. F. McDonald described the hurricane's track and intensity from birth to death:

> During the developing stage of the hurricane, as it was moving over remote islands and shoals of the southern Bahamas where there were no ships or island stations to report the passage of the small vortex, the problems of accurately locating the center and its line of advance and of forecasting its probable movement were extremely difficult. Nevertheless, timely and generally accurate advices were issued by the forecast center at Jacksonville, Fla., during this period. . . . [T]he progress of the hurricane northward and northeastward beyond the Florida Straits was fully covered by forecasts and timely warnings.

The last sentence was an artful one, combining as it did the storm's overland swath from Florida through Maryland with that initial, unforecast turn north from the Straits of Florida, tiny by comparison, yet so crucial to 400 veterans perched scant feet above sea level.

Having weathered the storm, the Bureau began developing and refining its forecasting procedures. Pan Am needed more precise weather information, which required more upper-air observations from the airline's clippers flying to and from South America, and more sea-level observations from ships plying the Atlantic and coastal waters. The Bureau also added more weather stations in the Caribbean.

In the next stage the Bureau set up warning stations along the Bahamas, and by 1944, airplanes—hurricane hunters—began flying into hurricanes. In the early 1960s, satellites began transmitting photographic images of hurricanes in motion. Today we have real-time imagery and evacuation procedures based on information from both satellites and from the radiosondes (instruments that broadcast humidity, temperature, and air pressure) that hurricane hunters drop inside the storms. But many Floridians now believe that the National Weather Service—as the government renamed the Weather Bureau in 1970—is too cautious, warning citizens to abandon their homes at the approach of the slightest tropical storm. The people who think that didn't live through the Great Labor Day Hurricane.

Climatologists say that global warming may well brew harsher, stronger storms in this century. As with the flu, we have no way of knowing how bad the next season will be.

———— ∞ ————

Not long after the storm, the railroad sent a ferryboat down to haul off Old 447, the relief train's engine. But the Florida Overseas Railway was never rebuilt; the bankrupt company sold the right-of-way for $640,000. It had cost Henry Flagler $27.2 million to build.

The veterans' camps were absorbed into the WPA that year as planned. Two and a half years later, on March 29, 1938, the road the veterans had started—the highway to Key

West—was opened. By 1943, engineers had redesigned and replaced the solid ramparts through the Upper Keys with bridges, allowing water to pass through the Keys instead of damming it up.

After the Depression, tourists flooded Key West, and a later president, Harry Truman, lived in what the press dubbed the Little White House on Front Street. The highway had an unexpected result. Before the railroad, and even in the twenty years after Flagler built it, each Key retained its own flavor. But the highway and the postwar generic chains that followed it homogenized the islands. The Matecumbe Hotel could never have been confused for the Long Key Fishing Camp, but Holiday Inns, Ramadas, Outback Steakhouses, Dairy Queens, and Winn-Dixies look the same everywhere. Yet the Florida Keys remain a culture unto themselves—easygoing, friendly, but laconic—offering no more than what you ask them, and sometimes even less.

<hr />

Ray Sheldon refused to return to government work but stayed in Florida; he started his own construction business and maintained his innocence until his death in 1952. Ghent became state director for the Resettlement Administration, and Van Hyning was made commissioner of social welfare for Florida. Julius Stone left government, attended Harvard Law School, and later became a real estate broker in Key West, his Gibraltar of the South. In 1958, in an effort to avoid taxes, he transferred holdings to Cuba with the support of President Batista. When Castro overthrew Batista the following year, Stone must have realized yet again how exquisitely poor his timing could be. He skipped the country in 1960 to avoid the Internal Revenue Service, landing in the Bahamas, then England. He died in 1967 in Australia. Ed Sheeran was disabled in a 1946 automobile accident and died in 1951. Like the first veterans removed from the Matecumbes, he was buried in Woodlawn Cemetery.

Ernest Hemingway's article in *New Masses* returned to haunt him decades later. "Who Murdered the Vets?" is never reprinted in any of his compilations, but that essay, along with his home in prerevolutionary Cuba and his anti-Fascist stance during the Spanish Civil War, would assure that the anti-Communist U.S. government of the 1950s would hound this rabid Republican in his twilight years. His prodigious drinking destroyed his health; his writing gift abandoned him. In the late 1950s he grew increasingly paranoid, and became convinced that men were following him. His paranoia led to electroshock therapy, and ultimately to his suicide by shotgun in his cabin in Ketchum, Idaho, in 1961. Yet his paranoia was well-founded. Sure of his Communist ties, government agents were, indeed, following him.

After Hemingway's death, Bernice Dickerson bought his home on Whitehead Street and turned it into a museum. It is now a registered National Historic Landmark. Tourists pay a fee and enter the once-private sanctum behind the uneven brick wall to traipse through the house and see Hemingway's possessions, books, and the descendants of his beloved six-toed cats; they stick their fingers in the saltwater swimming pool his wife, Pauline, had built for him in 1937; and they buy postcards and trinkets from a small shop set up in one of the rooms.

Sloppy Joe's remains a bar, now in its third Key West location, but it has also become a Hemingway museum of sorts; photos of him line the walls. Each year, Key West holds a Hemingway look-alike contest that brings in tourists by the thousands.

Hemingway would have been incensed.

Homestead, the haven for traumatized and injured vets in 1935, was nearly wiped off the map by Hurricane Andrew in 1992. In 2004 meteorologists upgraded Andrew a notch, from Category 4 to a 5. But the Great Labor Day Hurricane remains the champion, the most powerful storm of the twentieth century.

As for the veterans who survived this fiercest American hurricane, they just faded away as Douglas McArthur said old soldiers do. A fire in 1973 in the National Personnel Records Center in St. Louis destroyed their records, so we can only hope that men like Joseph "Frenchy" Fecteau lived the rest of their lives in peace, happiness, and prosperity, surrounded by loving families. Such an end is unlikely; life often doesn't work that way. Still, they deserved it. Frenchy deserved it.

On Sunday, November 14, 1937, more than two years after the storm, 5,000 people—government officials, guests, tourists, and even a few survivors—gathered around a canvas-draped monument on Islamorada. In FDR-era bureaucratese, the monument was officially known as Zone 3 Project Number 2217. Hugh Matheson deeded the land at Mile Marker 81.5 to the government in exchange for a patch of beachfront property to build a new school (the old one was destroyed in the hurricane), and the American Legion's Harvey Seeds Post of Miami raised $3,779 of its $12,000 final cost. The Florida Division of the Federal Art Project—a make-work program for artists—designed it, and the WPA built it. The "Shovel Leaners" dug its center down to the keystone bedrock and poured a stone-and-concrete base measuring 65 by 20 feet. That formed the crypt, where they placed the cremated remains of the dead. They covered that with a lid of keystone and placed an inlaid map of the Keys on top. Above it rises an 18-foot-high obelisk, also of keystone, with a design by Harold Lawson of tidal waves and palm trees bent by forceful winds. Nine-year-old Faye Marie Parker, one of the youngest survivors, unveiled it to the crowd. On a bronze plaque these words appear:

DEDICATED

TO THE MEMORY OF THE

CIVILIANS AND WAR VETERANS

WHOSE LIVES WERE LOST

IN THE HURRICANE OF

SEPTEMBER SECOND, 1935

S O U R C E S

MAGAZINES AND JOURNALS (IN CHRONOLOGICAL ORDER)

"Catastrophe: Wind, Water & Woe." *Time*, September 16, 1935.

Hemingway, Ernest. "Who Murdered the Vets? A First Hand Report on the Florida Hurricane." *New Masses*, September 17, 1935.

"Catastrophe: After the Storm." *Time*, September 23, 1935.

McDonald, W. F. "The Hurricane of August 31 to September 6, 1935." *Monthly Weather Review*, Vol. 63, No. 9, September 1935 (issued December 9, 1935).

"Rendezvous with Death." *The American Legion*, November 1935.

"Report of Special Investigating Committee, Florida Hurricane Disaster." *The American Legion*, November 1936.

"Fury in the Keys." *Tropic Magazine*, August 20, 1978.

NEWSPAPERS (IN CHRONOLOGICAL ORDER)

"Warning of Storm Ordered on Coast." *Miami Herald*, September 1, 1935.

"Liner *Dixie* Cast on Reef by Florida Hurricane with 400 Bound for N.Y." *New York Herald Tribune*, September 3, 1935.

"Family Afraid *Dixie* Skipper Will Go Down." *New York Herald Tribune*, September 4, 1935.

"Rescue Ships Standing by Liner on Reef." *Miami Herald*, September 4, 1935.

"Homestead People Are Swamped with Victims of Storm." *Miami Herald*, September 4, 1935.

"President Extends Army and Navy Aid." *Miami Herald*, September 4, 1935.

"Miami Guardsmen Ordered to Keys." *Miami Herald*, September 4, 1935.

"Veterans' Camp Wrecked by Storm." *Miami Herald*, September 4, 1935.

"Storm Toll in Keys Set at 25 to 100." *Miami Herald*, September 4, 1935.

"Woman Flier Sees 'No Signs of Life'." *Miami Herald*, September 4, 1935.

"Miami Police Arrange to Aid Identification." *Miami Herald*, September 4, 1935.

SOURCES

"Huge Wave Blamed for Deaths at Camp." *Miami Herald*, September 4, 1935.

"Report of 100 Dead at Tavernier Heard." *Miami Herald*, September 4, 1935.

"Inquiry Is Planned into Ship Grounding." *Miami Herald*, September 4, 1935.

"Trip 'Monotonous,' Passenger Wrote." *Miami Herald*, September 4, 1935.

"Wire Services Suffer South of Tampa Area." *Miami Herald*, September 4, 1935.

"Tender Will Go to Matecumbe." *Miami Herald*, September 4, 1935.

"Miamians Repairing Minor Storm Damage." *Miami Herald*, September 4, 1935.

"It's a Mild Hurricane, Weather Experts Assert." *New York Times*, September 5, 1935.

"Hundreds of Bodies Are Found in Wreckage on Florida Keys." *New York Times*, September 5, 1935.

"Veteran Says Camp Timbers, Matchsticks in Gale, Killed Many." *New York Times*, September 5, 1935.

"Passengers off SS *Dixie* Landed Here." *Miami Herald*, September 5, 1935.

"Investigation Asked of Disaster on Keys." *Miami Herald*, September 5, 1935.

SOURCES

"Pan-American Pilots View Storm Damage." *Miami Herald*, September 5, 1935.

"51 Rescued by Yacht from Veteran Camp 3." *Miami Herald*, September 5, 1935.

"Physician Describes 'Holocaust' on Keys." *Miami Herald*, September 5, 1935.

"Survivor Depicts Battle for Life." *Miami Herald*, September 5, 1935.

"200 to 500 Dead in Florida Hurricane." *New York Herald Tribune*, September 5, 1935.

"*Dixie* Passengers Smile Happily as They Land in Miami." *Miami Herald*, September 5, 1935.

"Tragic Storm Stories Related by Survivors." *Miami Herald*, September 5, 1935.

"Tired Workers Give Relief to Refugees." *Miami Herald*, September 5, 1935.

"Florida CCC Mobilize for Hurricane Relief." *Happy Days*, September 7, 1935.

"Legion Volunteers Give Heroic Service." *Miami Herald*, September 7, 1935.

"Governor Is Shocked by Scenes of Horror." *Miami Herald*, September 7, 1935.

"Hurricane Dead Are Ordered Cremated by Florida Governor." *Miami Herald*, September 7, 1935.

"Hurricane Wrecks Noted Fishing Spot." *Miami Herald*, September 7, 1935.

"Amateur Operators Link Keys With City." *Miami Herald*, September 7, 1935.

"Worley Absolves Railroad of Delay of Train to Camps." *Miami Herald*, September 7, 1935.

"Permanent Relief." *Miami Herald*, September 7, 1935.

"200 Workers Going into the Keys Today." *Miami Herald*, September 9, 1935.

"Storm Dead Are Honored in Park Rites." *Miami Herald*, September 9, 1935.

"Storm Death Toll Called Unavoidable." *Miami Herald*, September 9, 1935.

"Hurricane Victims Given Burial Here." *Miami Herald*, September 9, 1935.

"President Is Urged to Honor *Dixie* Crew." *Miami Herald*, September 9, 1935.

"New Investigation into Keys Disaster and Relief Sought." *Miami Herald*, September 11, 1935.

"Keys Residents Plan to Return to Old Lives." *Miami Herald*, September 11, 1935.

"Naming the Hurricane." *Miami Herald*, September 11, 1935.

"Hurricane Hits Florida Camp." *Happy Days*, September 14, 1935.

"Ship Officers Blameless in *Dixie* Wreck." *Miami Herald*, October 11, 1935.

"300 Storm Deaths Called Needless." *New York Times*, October 13, 1935.

"'Officials Deserted' in Storm, Is Charged." *Miami Herald*, October 15, 1935.

"Men in Key Camps Called 'Deserted'." *New York Times*, October 15, 1935.

"The Labor Day Hurricane of '35." *Islamorada Free Press*, August 31, 1988.

"Hurricane Survivors Recall Terror of '35." *Miami Herald*, September 2, 1991.

BOOKS

Barnes, Jay. *Florida's Hurricane History*. Chapel Hill: University of North Carolina Press, 1998.

Bartlett, John Henry. *The Bonus March and the New Deal*. Chicago, New York: M.A. Donohue & Co., 1937.

Bertsch, Werner J. *The Home and Museum of Ernest Hemingway*. Fort Lauderdale, Florida: Pro Publishing, 1999.

Bowditch, Nathaniel. *American Practical Navigator*. Pub. No. 9, Vol. 1. Defense Mapping Agency Hydrographic Center, 1977.

Carrier, Jim. *The Ship and the Storm: Hurricane Mitch and the Loss of the* Fantome. Camden, Maine: International Marine, 2001.

Cashman, Sean Dennis. *America in the Twenties and Thirties: The Olympian Age of Franklin Delano Roosevelt.* New York: New York University Press, 1989.

Davies, Pete. *Inside the Hurricane: Face to Face with Nature's Deadliest Storms.* New York: Henry Holt, 2000.

Dickson, Paul, and Thomas B. Allen. *The Bonus Army: An American Epic.* New York: Walker & Co., 2004.

Douglas, Marjorie Stoneman. *Hurricane.* New York: Rinehart, 1958.

Drye, Willie. *Storm of the Century: The Labor Day Hurricane of 1935.* Washington, D.C.: National Geographic Society, 2002.

Federal Writers' Project of the Works Progress Administration for the State of Florida. *Florida: A Guide to the Southern-Most State.* Sponsored by the state of Florida Department of Public Instruction. New York: Oxford University Press, 1939.

Hopkins, June. *Harry Hopkins: Sudden Hero, Brash Reformer.* New York: St. Martin's Press, 1999.

Leuchtenburg, William E. *Franklin D. Roosevelt and the New Deal, 1932–1940.* New York: Harper & Row, 1963.

Martin, Sidney Walter. *Henry Flagler: Visionary of the Gilded Age.* Lake Buena Vista, Florida: Tailored Tours Publications, 1998.

McIver, Stuart B. *Hemingway's Key West.* Sarasota, Florida: Pineapple Press, 1993.

SOURCES

Parks, Pat. *The Railroad That Died at Sea: The Florida East Coast's Key West Extension*. Brattleboro, Vermont: S. Greene Press, 1968.

Schlesinger, Arthur Meier. *The Coming of the New Deal: The Age of Roosevelt*. Vol. 2. Boston: Houghton Mifflin, 1988.

Sheets, Bob, and Jack Williams. *Hurricane Watch: Forecasting the Deadliest Storms on Earth*. New York: Vintage, 2001.

Standiford, Les. *Last Train to Paradise: Henry Flagler and the Spectacular Rise and Fall of the Railroad That Crossed the Ocean*. New York: Crown Publishers, 2002.

Watkins, T. H. *The Great Depression: America in the 1930s*. Boston: Little, Brown, 1993.

DOCUMENTS/REPORTS

Case Aides' Report of General Conditions Observed on Upper Keys from Matecumbe to Key West. Florida Emergency Relief Administration, Headquarters, District 9. Key West, Florida, September 16, 1935.

Florida Hurricane Disaster: Hearings Before the Committee on World War Veterans' Legislation. U.S. Congress. House. 74th Cong., 2nd sess. on H.R. 9486.

INTERNET SOURCES

www.flagler.org

www.keyshistory.org

INTERVIEWS

Eyster, Irving R., Keys historian.

McAllister, Mike, data acquisition program manager, Jacksonville National Weather Service.

McGrath, Larry, commander, Harvey W. Seeds Post No. 29, American Legion, Miami, Florida.

Wilkinson, Jerry, Keys historian, www.keyshistory.org.

Willoughby, Hugh, senior research meteorologist, Florida International University, Miami, Florida.

DEPOSITIONS
Camp 1

Anderson, E. A.
Anderson, James
Austin, Charles Reginald
Aycocks, W. D.
Bischweitz, Walter Joseph
Blair, W. M.
Boatman, Edgar
Bommer, Fred Jr.
Brady, Edward E.
Brannon, Clyde
Bridges, Ellis H.
Bryant, J. F.
Burchem, Charles
Burke, James M.

Carls, Robert
Chandler, Robert B.
Chandler, S. D.
Christie, Albert Earl
Clifford, John T.
Conrad, Thomas
Conway, John A.
Cook, Joseph
Coughlin, Peter P.
Cresse, Fred E.
Cunningham, J. J.
Davis, Albert V.
Davis, Stanley J.
Edgar, Frank
Edwards, Joe E.
Endicott, Byron

Esau, Wadie

Everett, Lloyd

Fatten, Peter

Ferguson, Hester

Fitchett, Lloyd Ray

Flow, Arnold B.

Fowler, John

Fox, Abraham

Frazer, Alexander

Friend, Robert D.

Frost, William H.

Fry, Oscar

Gaines, Hugh

Gallagher, Charles

Gallagher, Thomas J.

Gaskins, Harry

Gazley, James C.

Gottlieb [no first name given]

Grant, Edward

Hanley, Edward J.

Hardaker, William A.

Harris, Carl

Harris, Paul

Harrison, George M.

Harvey, James L.

Hatcher, Ira

Heintz, Frederick L.

Hellman, William A.

Herbert, Jacob S.

Higgins, Frank J.

Honor, Joe F.

Horton, Leone F.

Howard, Patrick

Howell, Tom S.

Huffman, Jackson M.

Huggins, John

Hurley, Roy R.

Ingham, Alfred John

Jacobs, David Edward

Jalonese, James

Jones, James R.

Jordan, P.

Kahn, Charles

Keith, Albert C.

Kelly, Hugh Joseph

Kerns, H. F.

King, Charles E.

King, James L.

Knowles, William

Kobal, Stanley Joseph

Krauss, Gus H.

Lamsarges, Ambrose

Larson, Peter C

Layman, Ray E.

LePreux, Raleigh

Lester, Roy

Long, Clarence H.

Lowkis, Eugene

Lydon, Joseph M.

Lynch, Jeremiah Joseph

Lyndon, Joseph M.

Magrady, Charles B.

Mahr, Philip Arthur

McAuley, Ernest E.

McAuley, Ernest W.

McCabe, John G.

McCloskey, Thomas

McComb, Everett A.

McDaniel, Hiram C.

McGrady, Charles B.

McGuire, A. M.

McLean, J. D.

McMullen, Leroy J.

McPherson, Robert J.

Miller, Lawrence M.

Moran, Leo A.

Morley, Clarence L.

Morris, John L.

Morrison, James C.

Morrison, James P.

Morrow, William

Mulholland, Robert A.
   [Hubert?]

Mullaney, Edward

Murray, Henry L.

Myers, Benjamin

Nabal, E. W.

Napier, E.

Nichols, Robert

O'Donnell, Loray

Oswald, Robert D.

Parker, Willard M

Pawa, Albert

Pitman, Mallie K.

Pope, Clay Henry

Prentiss, Guy

Raines, Grover C.

Richard, E. J.

Riley, John J.

Rogers, E. P.

Rooney, William L.

Rough, George

Rowe, Phil

Ruhland, John

Ryan, Jeremiah F.

Scanland, Owen

Scoggins, Gus L.

Scott, Loring

Senison, George Joseph

Shaw, Frank

Shea, James T.

Shipp, Robert Lee

Shropshire, Luther J.

Singleton, Eugene E.

Sipes, John W.

Smith, Chester

Smith, Odell

Smith, Walter

Snyder, Frederick F.

Stalnaker, Henry H.

Stanton, Harry P.

Suits, J. W.

Terry, William W.

Towles, John W.

Varnell, H. G.

Veal, Toulmine

Walsh, John

Wark, Samuel

Webb, Gordon V.

Weimann, Will J.

Wigginton, J. T.

Wynne, O. C.

Camp 3

Ballas, Frank M.

Barber, George D.

Barrett, W. F.

Beck, Harry

Bowen, James E.

Buckinger, Edward A.

Bonner [no first name given]

Brown, Arthur

Butts, John E.

Camp, Edward A.

Campbell, Anderson D.

Carey, John H.

Carter, Harry

Cawthon, Wilbur B.

Chambers, W. H.

Chatham, George D.

Coles, J. E.

Coward, Ben

Coyle, Kenneth

Cross, James E.

Crusoe, Joseph

Cushman, Harry J.

Darty, Elmer

Davis, Archie J.

Davis, John A.

Davis, Ben E.

Di Francisco, John

Dimitroff, Mike

Dombrauski, John

Donahue, Peter

Downs, Joseph Michael

Drybread, George

Eagan, Charles P.

Early, Thomas P.

SOURCES

Edwards, Clarence Burton

Einsig, C. M.

Ellis, Arthur

Ernest, Belote

Fahey, John P.

Fisher, John H.

Fleming, John

Fox, Earle L.

Gormely, Terence

Griffin, O. D.

Griffon, Peter

Grimes, Russell E.

Grubbs, R. O.

Guncheon, Clifford L.

Hagan, Charles P.

Hagan, William B.

Hanley, James

Harwood, Willard G.

Heckman, John Key

Hendrew, W. M.

Hicks, P. D.

Hilliard, John H.

Hovranko, Joseph

Johns, Dayton A.

Jones, Horace L.

Kelley, William J.

Kite, Louis D.

Kiwcnski, Chester

Klauss, Frank

Klein, William

Klock, William H.

Knox, William

Kohn, William

Kringer, A. F.

Lannon, Thomas F.

Larkin, Peter J.

Latach, Frank

Lederer, William

Lennon, James

Lindley, James B.

Machado, Anthony

Mahoney, Edward J.

Mallon, John J.

McCain, Clyde

McClary, Charles

McClintic, French E.

McDermott, Michael

McDonough, Francis J.

McMannus, Arthur

McNamara, L. W.

Meyers, I. L.

Miller, Edwin William

Miller, Junius

Morris, O.N.H.

Mullen [no first name given]

Nash, Thomas J.

Nibouar, John

Nonnenman, Jacob

O'Brien, Lawrence J.

Parkinson, Tom G.

Perdue, Samuel A.

Perhack, Matthew

Perry, Cornelius J.

Pfister, Andrew J.

Phillips, Clifford M.

Postell, Gay Marion

Pugh, Paul

Rambowski, Adam

Riddell, Lewis

Ringer, James

Ritchie, Edward C.

Roach, Earle

Ross, William F.

Rumage, De Forrest

Sacks, Jacob

Saibel, John H.

Sain, C. G.

Schadt, Justus

Schroeder, William

Sharp, Robert A.

Shockley, Lester

Silve, Ira

Skularicos, John

Smith, George

Smith, Harry

Sowerby, George S.

Sullivan, Robert

Tapp, Morris R.

Taylor, J. W.

Thilmann, Albert

Tiller, Thomas E.

Tischenbach, Frank R.

Trombetta, Joseph

Warfield, James T.

Warren, William A.

Wells, Luther

Whittaker, Raymond

Widmeyer, Gordon A.

Wilshire, Herbert S.

Wojtkiewicz, Joseph

Camp 5

Africa, Quinton

Allen, Leslie D.

Bailey, Chester A.

Belk, William S.

Bowman, Thomas D.

Bradfield, B. L.

Branscum, Russell

Buck, Albert

Byers, Dexter V.

Condry, Martin M.

Cunningham, Eugene E.

Cuthbertson, Ernest M.

Earl, James Francis

Fecteau, Joseph

Goodman, Virgil C.

Haggerty, Virgil

Harrod, Frank B.

Hill, George T.

Hogan, Maurice F.

Hughes, Frank J.

Hytte, Arbie

Jedrack, Joseph

Jerrell, Melton

Kordel, Karl H.

Lapinski, Tony

Lavett, E. R.

Linawik, Gus

Macdonald, Jay

Maloney, George A.

Martin, Turner K.

Martin, William Kenneth

Meade, Arbie

Medlin, Oscar R.

Mills, Allen

Morris, Hollis

Mulholland, Hubert A.

Neely, Vernon G.

Poock, Frederick

Romanowski, Steve R.

Simoni, Frank H.

Smith, Robert L.

Storey, John

Tallent, Clarence

Thompson, William R.

Trafka, Walter J.

Tucker, Nathan

Vasakosky, Frank J.

Wall, James A.

Walters, Alexander

Willis, Clarence A.

Administration and Civilians

Alexander, Lassiter, M.D.

Ayer, Robert Aldrich Jr.

Baker, Harry W.

Bennett, Walter J.

Bilsbrough, Arthur P.

Bow, Richard Lawrence

Burris, W. Z.

Butters, Ed

Carson, Ernest

Combs, J. R.

Delaplante, A. W.

Duncan, B. M.

Dunn, Gordon E.

Evers, Willis William
Fritchman, L. A.
Ghent, Fred B.
Good, John
Harrell, Thomas B.
Huau, Joseph Hipolito
Hughes, Charlotte
Johns, William M.
Johnson, Rufus B.
Jones, Wilbur E.
King, O. D.
Knabel, H. F.
Maloney, Louis
Melcolm, D. A.
Mewshaw, Arthur Williams
Nichols, Hubert Campbell
Parker, E. B.
Pattison, Eugene A.
Perdue, Olin
Pervis, Jones A.
Russell, John A.
Sheeran, Edward H.
Smith, Wilton Lindsey
Thompson, Karl O.
Unkrich, R. C.

Vander Schouw, Paul
Van Hyning, Conrad
Van Vechten, Charles W.
Wiggington, Junius Talbutt

Camp Unknown

Clarkson, John C.
Ford, John H.
Glisson, Hayward E.
Harrell, Thomas B.
Irwin, William E.
Johnson, Robert C. A.
Jwalsky, Walter
Kubiak, John J.
Mayhew, Charles
McGeady, Joseph F.
McNulty, John T.
Parks, Claude W.
Rice, Walter R.
Ringer, James V.
Singletary, Charles
Traynor, Robert
Voyles, Philip
White, Fred B.

ACKNOWLEDGMENTS

Thanks to Dr. Joe Castanza, for his continuous advice on the science of storms; editor Jonathan Eaton, whose attention to detail made this book what it is; copyeditor Peter Weissman, project editor Margaret Cook, and art director Molly Mulhern; Krista Scott for research, editing, and proofreading; the staff of the National Archives, and especially Gene Morris; Tom Hambright for his help at the Key West Public Library; Jim Norris, Brian Nash, Peter Engelman, and Jo Fritts for proofreading and comments; Pat Trenner, Perry Turner, and Carmine Infantino for their continued support; and Jerry Wilkinson, Florida Keys historian and the driving force behind www.keyshistory.org, whose review of the manuscript and help with photo research were timely and invaluable and who is not responsible for any errors that remain. He is also spearheading the effort to honor the contributions and sacrifices of the World War I veterans in the Keys by naming the small island that has developed from the

ACKNOWLEDGMENTS

remains of the proposed bridge from Lower Matecumbe Key to Fiesta Key Veterans Key. For more information, go to www.keyshistory.org. And finally, thanks to Kitty, Kitty II, Kitty III, and Turtle. The first was around long before the proposal and succumbed during the research, the second lived through much of the writing, and the other two got me through the final chapters and the revisions. Thanks, girls.